THE ROOF OF THE WORLD

Exploring the Mysteries of the Qinghai-Tibet Plateau

THE ROOF OF

By Zhang Mingtao and Other Members of the Multidisciplinary Research

Harry N. Abrams, Inc., New York, and

THE WORLD

Team of the Qinghai-Tibet Plateau, Chinese Academy of Sciences

Foreign Languages Press, Beijing

Project Director: Margaret L. Kaplan
Designer: Bob McKee
Copy Editor: Donn Teal

Library of Congress Cataloging in Publication Data
Zhang, Mingtao.
    The roof of the world.
    Includes index.
    1. Tibet (China)—Description and travel—Views.
2. Tsinghai Province (China)—Description and travel—Views.
I. Chung-kuo k'o hsüeh yüan. Multidisciplinary Research Team
on the Qinghai-Tibet Plateau.   II. Title.
DS786.Z46   951'.47   81-1269
ISBN 0-8109-1558-8   AACR2

©1982 Foreign Languages Press, Beijing

Printed and bound in Japan

Frontispiece spread: Karila glacier, on a peak 6,500 meters above sea
level in southern Tibet.

CONTENTS

EDITOR'S NOTE

The Qinghai-Tibet Plateau, in southwest China, is sometimes called "the roof of the world." It is one of the few remaining places on earth that have not yet been fully explored by man.

Covering more than 2.2 million square kilometers, this vast tableland is the largest of its kind in the world. It extends from the Kunlun Mountains in the north to the Himalayas in the south, and from the Karakorum Range in the west to the Hengduan Mountains in the east. It is also the highest plateau on earth, with an average elevation of 4,500 meters above sea level and more than 3,000 meters above the surrounding plains and basins. Moreover, it is the youngest geologic phenomenon on the globe, part of it having been lifted out of the sea only 40 million years ago.

Scientists have long been fascinated by the mysteries of the Qinghai-Tibet Plateau. What mighty force could have raised so huge a part of the earth's crust, creating this incomparable landscape? What cataclysmic changes took place during its formation? What impact has the existence of the Plateau had on the natural environment? And, above all, what resources does it hold and how can they be exploited for man's benefit?

In an attempt to answer some of these questions, Chinese scientists began research in the area in the 1950s. The first explorations were limited and sporadic, owing to insufficient trained personnel and lack of funds. By the early 1970s, however, it had become possible to undertake more ambitious expeditions. Thanks to a new emphasis on the study of modern science in China, large numbers of researchers had been trained. In addition, the government was prepared to support large-scale research: it needed accurate information on which to base projects to develop the area and improve the life of the inhabitants. Accordingly, the Chinese Academy of Sciences embarked upon a "program of Multidisciplinary Research on the Qinghai-Tibet Plateau for 1973–1980."

Time and time again the research team's trucks got stuck in the soggy earth of the North Tibet plateau. It was exhausting labor to free the wheels, especially since the team was working in the rarefied air that makes any physical exertion difficult.

In the course of the program, the Academy sent more than 400 researchers to the Tibet Autonomous Region. They included specialists in geophysics, geology, geography, biology, agriculture, forestry, and animal husbandry, drawn from schools, research institutes, and production organizations all over China. The specialists were assisted by residents of the area, who served as guides and provided transport and support services, as well as by soldiers of the People's Liberation Army, who helped in the research work.

On their expeditions to the Plateau, the scientific teams investigated exceedingly varied terrain, trekking over snowcapped mountains and glaciers, crossing rivers and lakes, exploring volcanoes, penetrating subtropical forests, and traversing rich pastures and farmland. This book, a work of collective effort, was written by some of the research team members themselves: Chapter 3, Frozen Wonderland, by Li Jijun of Lanzhou University; Chapter 8, Alpine Plants, by Wu Sugong of the Institute of Botany, Chinese Academy of Sciences; and the rest by Zhang Mingtao, a geothermal specialist of the Commission on the Comprehensive Survey of Natural Resources of China, Chinese Academy of Sciences, who also contributed the second-largest number of photographs reproduced in this volume. In the course of his work writing eleven chapters of the book, he consulted the expert advice of his colleagues in the Academy: Li Wenhua, Han Yufeng, Huang Wenxiu, and Li Jiyou of the Commission on the Comprehensive Survey of Natural Resources; Feng Zuojian of the Institute of Zoology; Chang Chengfa and Zheng Xilan of the Institute of Geology; Teng Jiwen of the Institute of Geophysics; and Zhang Yongzu, Zheng Du, and Li Bingyuan of the Institute of Geography. Chen Heyi, editor of *China Pictorial* magazine, helped in the editorial work and contributed the greatest number of photographs to be used for the book. The names of all the photographers whose pictures appear herein are given in the list of Photo Credits. The maps and diagram were drawn by Zhang Mingtao, Shen Peilong, Zu Yuting, Zheng Du, and Teng Yufang.

As we go to press, we learn with deep sorrow that Zheng Changlu, a *China Pictorial* correspondent who contributed many photographs for this album, died in an accident in the summer of 1981 while going on an expedition with the scientific research team to the Hengduan Mountains in Yunnan. He had joined three expeditions to the Qinghai-Tibet Plateau before his untimely death at the age of thirty-seven.

BAI YAN

1 GEOGRAPHY OF THE PLATEAU

The Qinghai-Tibet Plateau is composed of a number of distinct regions, each with dramatically different topography.

Along the southern edge of the Plateau, extending for 2,400 kilometers from west to east, is the greatest mountain range on earth: the stupendous Himalayas, 6,000 to 7,000 meters above sea level. At the center of the range, locked in snow and ice, are clustered eleven of the world's fourteen loftiest peaks, including Qomolangma (Mount Everest), which at 8,848.13 meters is the highest point on the globe. The range declines gradually from the center in both directions, until at each tip there rises another mighty peak. At the western end stands Mount Nanga-parbat, in Kashmir, with the Indus River at its feet. At the eastern end is Mount Namjagbarwa, in China, with the Yarlung Zangbo (Zangbo means river in Tibetan)—the upper Brahmaputra—looping around it.

1. The Qinghai-Tibet Plateau seen on a terrestrial globe.

The ridgeline of the Himalayas forms a definite line of demarcation, with a different climate and different plant and animal life on either side of the range. The mountain mass blocks most of the warm, moisture-laden air of the Indian Ocean from reaching the interior of the Plateau. For this reason, the south face of the Himalayas has a warm, humid climate and verdant vegetation, while the north face of the range and much of the rest of the Plateau is frigid and arid. On the south side, the abundant rainfall and the surface flow of water it creates cause heavy erosion on the precipitous slopes, and the bigger rivers cut deep gorges between the mountains.

These river gorges represent shortcuts through the Himalayas, but they are so nearly impassable that local travelers prefer to cross over the perilous mountain passes, where the air is thin and ice and snow block the way eight months of the year. Our research team, however, chose the valley routes, following the course of the roaring rivers. When a gorge became too narrow, we climbed the steep walls with ropes and picks and threaded our way through the dense forests until we could descend to another section of the river valley. In this way, we were able to study the various types of vegetation and wildlife, the waterpower resources, and the geologic strata preserved intact on the canyon walls.

Not far from the foot of the north face of the Himalayas, and roughly parallel to them, is a belt of undulating mountains that the Tibetans call the Lhagoi Kangris. This elongated range forms a watershed, dividing the Yarlung Zangbo water system to the north and the Ganges water system to the south. On both sides of the watershed, the erosion of the rivers has broken down the banks of many of the big lakes, draining them of water and carving ravines into the dried-up basins.

Between the Lhagoi Kangri Mountains and another, parallel range to the north, the Gangdise-Nyainqentanglhas, lies the valley of South Tibet. Near the western end of the valley is one of the scenic wonders of Tibet: inside a ring of mountains, whose peaks are covered with snow and glaciers, lie two shimmering freshwater lakes, the Mapam Yumco and the Langa. This beautiful basin, with its twin lakes surrounded by rich pastureland, is held sacred by the Buddhists as the blessed abode of the gods, and countless pilgrims are drawn to it not only from the Tibet Autonomous Region but also from India, Nepal, Sikkim, and Bhutan.

The lake basin is of special interest for another reason. In the surrounding mountains lie the headwaters of three of the principal rivers of the South Asian subcontinent: the Indus, the Ganges, and the Brahmaputra. The largest and most important of these upper rivers is the Yarlung Zangbo (upper Brahmaputra). The highest big river in the world, it flows from west to east, more or less parallel to the Himalayas. Near the twin lakes, the valley is flat-bottomed, and the river spreads out in a network of wandering channels that water a luxuriant pastureland. Here roam great herds of yaks and flocks of sheep.

Farther east, down the middle reaches of the Yarlung Zangbo, the valley drops in elevation and alternately narrows and widens. In the narrow sections, the river races through steep gorges rich in rare mineral deposits, and the swift-flowing water is a great potential source of power. Where the valley broadens, and along the lower reaches of the tributary streams feeding into the river from the north and south, the land is fertile and densely populated. Lhasa, the largest city in Tibet and the capital of the Autonomous Region, is built on the banks of one of these tributaries, the Lhasa River. This part of the valley of South Tibet is the highest agricultural region on earth, yet bountiful crops of wheat and barley and thriving orchards of apples, peaches, and walnuts belie the fact that they perch on "the roof of the world."

In the southeastern end of the valley, the river makes a horse-shoe loop around Mount Namjagbarwa at the tip of the Himalayas before it leaves the Qinghai-Tibet Plateau and eventually becomes the Brahmaputra River in India. Here the land comes down to less than 3,000 meters above sea level. Warm, humid air from the Indian Ocean moves up the river valley, so that the region has lush vegetation, including an enormous forest zone.

To the north of the South Tibet Valley there rise two more huge mountain ranges, the Gangdise and the Nyainqentanglha. These ranges form a watershed which, with the exception of a few rivers, divides the exterior drainage system of South Tibet and the inland drainage system of North Tibet. Thus it is an important geographic line of demarcation.

On the other side of the Gangdise and the Nyainqentanglha mountains lies the vast heartland of Tibet, known as the North Tibet plateau. This region consists of a series of narrow lake basins and river valleys separated by tremendous mountain ranges, including the Tanggulas, the Karakorum, the Hohxil, and the Kunlun, which last forms the northern border of the Qinghai-Tibet Plateau. Viewed from the Plateau, these mighty ranges, among the highest in the world, do not appear as elevated as they actually are. However, when the scientific research team climbed the Kunlun Mountains from the Tarim Basin just north of the Plateau, we found the feat as arduous as the ascent of the Himalayas from the south.

There is no real summer on the North Tibet plateau. Even in the warm season of July and August, a snowstorm may strike, and the temperature at night sometimes drops below freezing. Alternating extremes of temperature cause the topsoil to freeze and thaw repeatedly. The resulting contraction and expansion of the soil creates a natural sorting process in which the coarser gravel is squeezed down into cracks in the ground, forming curious geometric patterns.

Considering these rugged conditions, one might expect the North Tibet plateau to be utterly barren, but for a number of reasons the region is one of the few highest in the world where vegetation exists. Three feet underground is a layer of permafrost that is impenetrable to meltwater from the surface and therefore keeps the topsoil moist. The thin, clear atmosphere permits intense solar radiation, and this also favors plant growth during the brief warm season. Lastly, the plateau is dotted with lakes, including Lake Nam, or Nam Co, the highest and largest lake in Tibet, with an area of some 2,000 square kilometers. Both the freshwater lakes like the Nam, which are surrounded with vegetation, and the salt lakes, whose silvery borders are bare of life, serve to temper the harsh climate.

When the weather clears in the warm season, the North Tibet plateau presents a panorama of extraordinary beauty. Amid the still silence of the shimmering lakes and sun-gilded volcanic rock ridges, dormant life reawakens. After withstanding violent gales and freezing cold, the dwarfed but hardy alpine plants burst into gorgeous bloom and complete their life cycle in the short growing season. Flocks of migrating birds glide across the sky and skim over the lakes, while herds of wild asses and gazelles gallop on the lakeside meadows. (Sometimes the members of our research team hunted Mongolian gazelles to provide a welcome change in the team's diet.)

To the east, the North Tibet plateau extends into neighboring Qinghai Province. The terrain here is similar to that in the west, but the altitude is generally lower and the climate more hospitable, so the area is somewhat more densely populated. China's two largest rivers, the Changjiang (Yangtze) and the Huanghe (Yellow), originate in this part of the Plateau, as does also the Lancang, which becomes the Mekong, the most important river of Indochina.

In the southeast, where the Qinghai-Tibet Plateau takes in parts of Sichuan and Yunnan provinces as well, the topography is very different. There are no wide valleys and lake basins, as in the west. Here, among parallel rows of craggy mountains, the Nujiang, Lancang, and Jinsha rivers have cut steep canyons, sometimes 2,000 to 3,000 meters deep. It took our research team half a day to travel on the Sichuan-Tibet highway from one

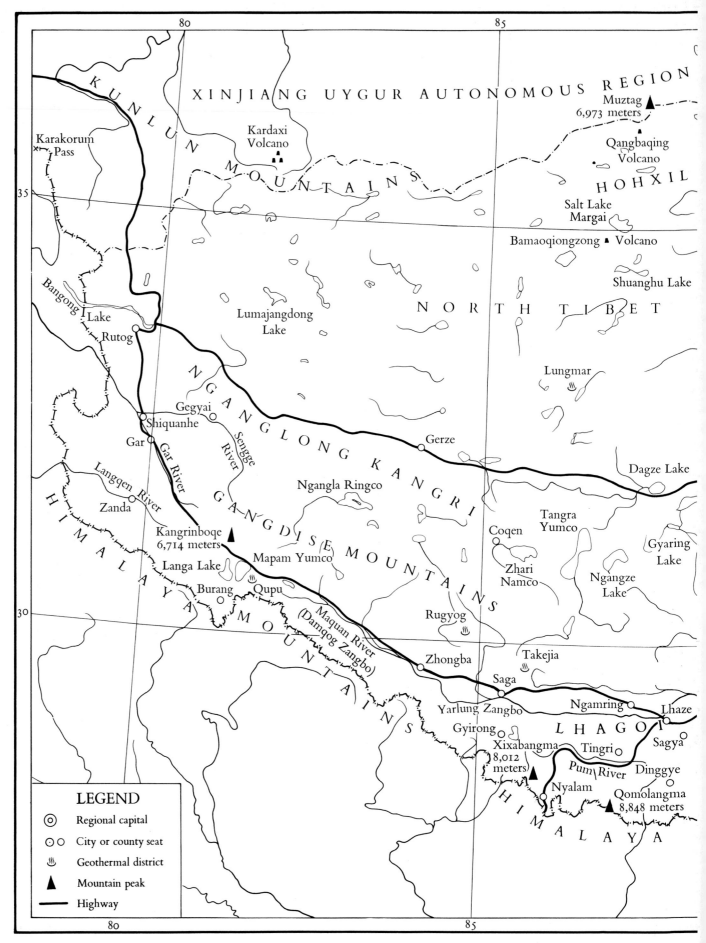

MAP OF THE
QINGHAI-TIBET
PLATEAU

KUNLUN MOUNTAINS

XINJIANG UYGUR AUTONOMOUS REGION

Muztag
6,973 meters

Qangbaqing
Volcano

Kardaxi
Volcano

HOHXIL

Karakorum
Pass

35

Salt Lake
Margai

Bamaoqiongzong ▲ Volcano

Shuanghu Lake

NORTH TIBET

Bangong Lake

Lumajangdong
Lake

Rutog

Lungmar

NGANGLONG KANGRI

Gegyai

Shiquanhe

Gerze

Sengge River

Gar

Dagze Lake

Gar River

Langqen River

Ngangla Ringco

GANGDISE MOUNTAINS

Zanda

Coqen

Tangra
Yumco

Kangrinboqe
6,714 meters

Gyaring
Lake

Mapam Yumco

Zhari
Namco

Ngangze
Lake

Langa Lake

Burang

Qupu

Rugyog

Maquan River
(Damqog Zangbo)

30

HIMALAYA MOUNTAINS

Zhongba

Takejia

Saga

Ngamring

Lhaze

Yarlung Zangbo

Gyirong

LHAGO

Xixabangma
8,012
meters

Tingri

Sagya

Pum River

Dinggye

Nyalam

Qomolangma
8,848 meters

HIMALAYA

LEGEND
◎ Regional capital
○○ City or county seat
♨ Geothermal district
▲ Mountain peak
── Highway

80

85

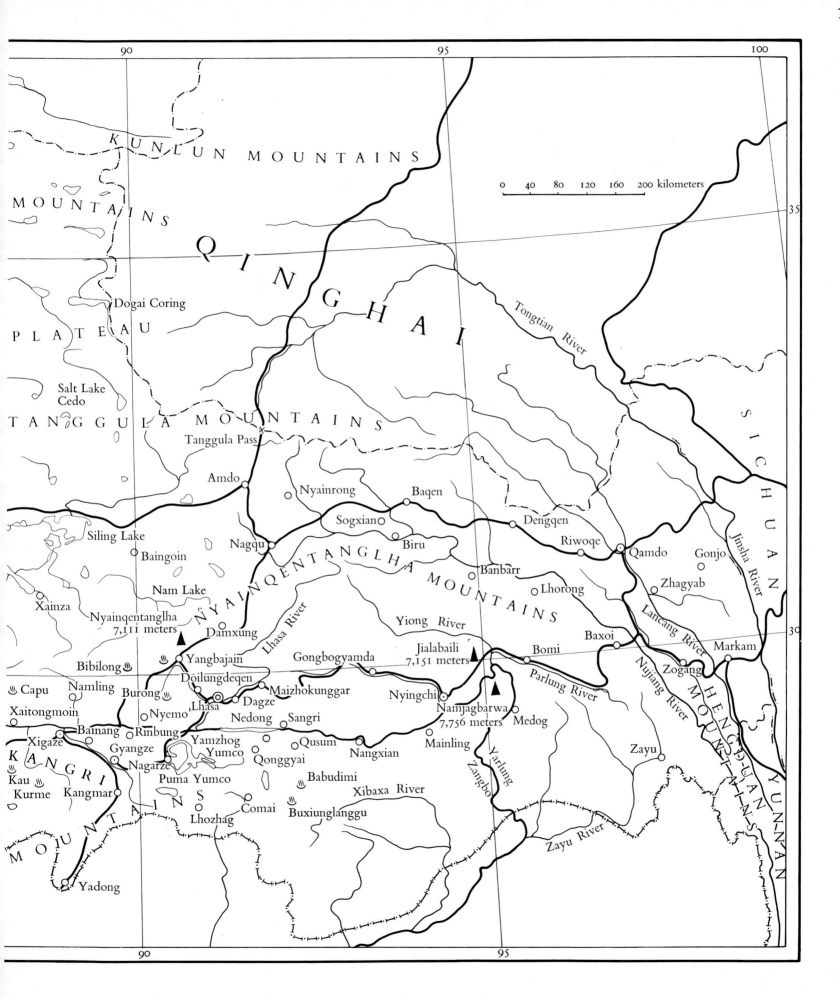

KUNLUN MOUNTAINS

MOUNTAINS

QINGHAI

0 40 80 120 160 200 kilometers

35

Dogai Coring

PLATEAU

Salt Lake
Cedo

TANGGULA MOUNTAINS

Tongtian River

SICHUAN

Tanggula Pass

Amdo

Nyainrong

Baqen

Dengqen

Sogxian

Riwoqe

Siling Lake

Nagqu

Biru

Qamdo

Gonjo

Baingoin

Banbarr

Lhorong

Zhagyab

Jinsha River

Nam Lake

NYAINQENTANGLHA MOUNTAINS

Xainza

Yiong River

Baxoi

Lancang River

30

Nyainqentanglha
7,111 meters ▲ Damxung

Lhasa River

Jialabaili
7,151 meters ▲

Bomi

Markam

Bibilong ♨

♨ Yangbajain

Gongbogyamda

Parlung River

Zogang

Nujiang River

HENGDUAN

Namling

Doilungdeqen

Nyingchi

♨ Capu

Burong ♨

Maizhokunggar

Xaitongmoin

♨ Lhasa Dagze

Nedong

Sangri

Namjagbarwa
7,756 meters Medog

Mainling

Zayu

YUNNAN

Nyemo

Bainang Rinbung

Qusum

Nangxian

Xigaze

Gyangze

Yamzhog
Yumco

Zayu River

KANGRI

Nagarze

Qonggyai

Yarlung

MOUNTAINS

Kau ♨

Puma Yumco

♨ Babudimi

Zangbo

Kurme Kangmar

Xibaxa River

S

Comai

♨ Buxiunglanggu

Lhozhag

MOUNTAINS

Yadong

90

95

100

90

95

mountaintop to another, driving circuitously down one slope, crossing a roaring river, then zigzagging to the top of the next, where still we saw no end to the retreating rows of towering mountains. Viewed from one of the crests, the undulating ridgelines block the intervening chasms from sight and seem to form a rolling plain—a replica of the original surface of the Plateau before it was cut by the rivers.

Unlike most of China's mountain chains, which run from west to east, the mountains in this southeastern portion of the Plateau extend from north to south and are therefore known as the Hengduan or "traversing" mountains. The Hengduan Range presents more than scientific interest for man. Thanks to the monsoons from the Indian Ocean and the South Pacific, which advance north along the river valleys bringing warmth and rain, the upper levels of the mountainsides are covered with dense forests, while the lower slopes are striped with bands of terraced rice, wheat, and corn. Some of the southern valleys even have a subtropical climate in which sugarcane, citrus fruits, and bananas can be grown. The narrow mountain gorges hold promise of enormous hydropower, and the whole area is rich in mineral deposits. Thus, far from being a uniform, desolate wasteland, as is commonly supposed, the Qinghai-Tibet Plateau offers a wealth of varied natural resources.

2. The average height of the Himalayas is 6,000 meters above sea level on the southern border of the Plateau. The most prodigious mountains on earth, they attract many mountaineers and scientists.

3

3. The Langqen River valley in South Tibet. The river meanders in a network of braided channels, a typical feature of the wide river valleys here.

4. The racing Nujiang River cuts 2,000 to ➤ 3,000 meters down the Hengduan Range, making this typical V-shaped canyon. The peasants are harvesting buckwheat on the steep hillsides. On the lower slopes, where the land is more fertile, terraced crops can be seen.

5

5. The Parlung River, a tributary of the
Yarlung Zangbo in the eastern part of the
South Tibet Valley. In this region the climate
is warm and humid and the land is fertile. The
field in the foreground has been sown to
wheat.

6

7

6. The Gyirong River, flowing across the China–Nepal border, cuts deeply into the still-rising Himalayas to form this canyon. Its smaller tributaries, with less cutting force, often remain at a higher level and join the river in the form of waterfalls like the one shown here.

7. A river gorge in the western part of the South Tibet Valley. The rock walls, bare of vegetation in this arid region, are severely weathered by extremes of temperature.

8

8. Mount Kangrinboqe, 6,714 meters in elevation, is the main peak of the Gangdise Range. It is made of stratified conglomerates that were formed early in the Tertiary period and later elevated. The Tibetan people regard it as a sacred mountain because of its unusual cone shape, the result of erosion by ice and snow.

9

9. The Karakorum Mountains on the North Tibet plateau. The main peak of this range, Mount Qogir, which stands outside the Qinghai-Tibet Plateau to the northwest, is second in elevation only to Qomolangma (Mount Everest). It is 8,611 meters above sea level.

11

12

10. The Nyainqentanglha mountain chain amidst a sea of clouds. This range, whose main peak is 7,111 meters above sea level, is actually the northeast extension of the Gangdises. North of the Nyainqentanglhas is the parallel Tanggula Range; "Nyainqentanglha" means "the second Tanggula" in Tibetan.

11. Mount Muztag, at 6,973 meters above sea level, is the main peak of the Kunlun chain, which forms the northern border of the Qinghai-Tibet Plateau. Viewed from the North Tibet plateau, itself more than 5,000 meters in elevation, the lofty Kunlun Mountains appear to be of only moderate height.

12. On the vast North Tibet plateau, 4,600 to 5,200 meters above sea level, valleys and lake basins lie between parallel mountain ranges whose general direction is from west to east.

14

13. The weather on the North Tibet plateau is unpredictable. Here a snowstorm has struck the camp of the research team in July.

14. The Damqog, upper river of the Yarlung Zangbo, wanders over a section of primeval tableland. Because the land is flat and the river flows slowly with little cutting force, there are no terraces along the banks.

15. Getting ready for the day's journey, despite the August snow on the North Tibet plateau.

15

17

16. On the hilly land of the North Tibet plateau are pastures consisting mainly of needlegrass.

17. With the exception of a few higher peaks, the Hengduan Mountains are generally about 4,500 meters above sea level. Viewed from the top, the ridgelines seem to form a continuous surface reaching to the horizon.

HISTORY OF THE PLATEAU

Man has achieved much in the scientific field, but his understanding of this world is still far from complete. Earth's formation, the genesis of life itself, and phenomena such as the Bermuda Triangle remain mysteries even to this day. One major question that has caught the attention of geologists throughout the world is the origin of the Qinghai-Tibet Plateau, which some regard as the key to the enigma of crustal dynamics—the science of matter and motion in the earth's crust. In order to understand the formation of the Plateau, we must first briefly consider the basic composition of this planet as a whole.

The earth is structured rather like an egg and consists fundamentally of three spherical shells. Outermost is a thin, rocky crust, enveloping a comparatively thick layer, or mantle, which in turn encompasses a central core. The crust, composed mainly of layers of granite and basalt, has an average thickness of 35 kilometers below the continents, but a mere 5 to 8 kilometers below the oceans. The mantle, which constitutes the greater part of the earth's bulk, has a dividing line 1,000 kilometers below the earth's surface, separating it into the upper and lower mantles. Within the upper mantle is a layer of low seismic velocity, about 60 to 150 kilometers thick. This is known as the asthenosphere. The temperature of this layer is extremely high and approaches the melting point of the substances present in it. Above the asthenosphere lies a strong surface layer of rock called the lithosphere, broken into plates of varying sizes. These plates are in constant motion, because they are affected by tectonic movements—movements which create folds and breaks in the crustal rocks. It is vigorous activity of this kind within the lithosphere and the asthenosphere that has played a major role in lifting up the Qinghai-Tibet Plateau.

Our scientific team included specialists in almost every branch of the earth sciences to study the upheaval of the Plateau. As we collected specimens, sifted data, and performed experiments, our discoveries constantly made us modify or totally revise former views.

One of the first tasks we set ourselves was to determine the force of the gravitational field in the area, so that we could calculate the approximate thickness of the earth's crust and its state of equilibrium.

1

1. A drawing of the *Changdusaurus*, which lived toward the end of the mid-Jurassic period. The animal stood about three meters high and measured almost seven meters in length.

2. In the Jurassic period, 150 million years ago, the area about the North Tibet plateau and the Hengduan mountain region had already risen above the sea and was inhabited by dinosaurs. Here we see the western slopes of the Darma La Mountains, in Qamdo Prefecture, site of the *Changdusaurus* fossil.

2

Any landmass can be likened to a block of wood floating on water, of which the part above the water's surface is supported by the buoyancy of the part below it. With a larger block of wood, the section exposed above the water will be greater and the portion submerged will be correspondingly deeper. This is Archimedes' Principle of Equilibrium. According to this principle, since the Qinghai-Tibet Plateau is the highest-lying piece of land on earth, with an average elevation of 4,000 to 5,000 meters above sea level, the depth of the crust pressed down into the mantle beneath it must be greater than that usually found under the continents. It was in fact found to measure 70 kilometers in the central part of the Plateau, almost twice the normal thickness beneath continents. This can be explained by the fact that the density of the earth's crust is 10 to 20 percent less than the mantle under it. It has been verified that, in general, the thickness of the crust beneath the Plateau is exactly in a state of equilibrium with the height of the Plateau above sea level.

What puzzled us initially, however, was that Qomolangma (Everest), whose peak towers more than 8,000 meters above sea level, lies above a crust only 50 kilometers thick. Obviously, the "buoyancy" forces exerted by the crust pressing into the mantle at this point are insufficient to support such a huge mountain mass. But it would be wrong to suppose that the mountain is sinking. On the contrary, surveys have proved that, in fact, the whole Himalayan Range is rising. Its upward movement must therefore depend on extremely powerful forces pressing in from the sides. We set up stations on both the north and south side of the Himalayas to keep a continuous record of seismic activity in the area, and analysis of the seismic waves confirmed that tremors in the southern part of the Plateau were indeed caused mainly by north-south or northeast-southwest horizontal compression.

Our seismologists also set off a series of underwater explosions in the deep lakes on the Plateau—in and around Lake Yamzhog Yumco, for example—thus creating elastic waves, capable of resisting compression. By studying the propagation of these waves in different underground rock strata, we were able to study the deeper parts of the Plateau's structure. The figures we obtained corresponded with those developed by the gravitation method mentioned above. The tests revealed that the crust and upper mantle under the Plateau is of multilayered composition and that the area undergoing the most rapid structural changes is located in the southern part of the Plateau, where earthquakes are frequent and hydrothermal activity is extremely violent.

We also carried out paleomagnetic research. Available evidence shows that, throughout the course of the earth's development, the positions of the paleomagnetic poles have changed considerably—have indeed reversed many times. Igneous rocks and certain sedimentary rocks at the time of their formation incorporated some substances that were subsequently magnetized by the earth's field. Many of these rocks still retain their magnetism. As fossils do by their location, this magnetism provides a geochronology of the layers and the rocks, and is therefore referred to as "fossil magnetism." This magnetism records the condition of the layers and the rocks during certain geologic periods; and consequently the positions of the geomagnetic poles relative to the locations of the rocks can be inferred.

Any landmass that originally belonged to the same single continental or oceanic crust will have identical positions of paleomagnetic poles of a certain geologic era, as represented by the magnetization of a succession of rocks in them, though the landmass may have drifted to another part of the globe. Consequently, the relative shifting of different landmasses in various geologic eras can be ascertained by studying the magnetism left in rocks.

3

4

3. Site of the fossils of Cathaysian flora: Shuanghu, northern Tibet. In the North Tibet plateau and the Hengduan mountain region on the eastern part of the Qinghai-Tibet Plateau were found large quantities of fossil Cathaysian flora, which lived 200 million years ago in the Permian period. This shows that long ago this region and the eastern part of China were one continent.

4. Fossils of the three-toed *Hipparion*, which lived 10 million years ago, have been found in the Gyirong basin in southern Tibet and the Bulung basin in northern Tibet. The climate in these basins then was warm and humid. Here we see a site where fossils of ancient animal bones were found in the Gyirong basin.

5. A volcanic cone in the Kaerda volcanic cluster on the northern periphery of the North Tibet plateau.

Our team took rock samples from the same geologic horizon both north of the Yarlung Zangbo and at other places on the Eurasian continent and found that the positions of the magnetic poles were generally the same. However, the magnetism recorded in rocks of corresponding geologic eras taken in India, to the south of the Plateau, differed markedly. This indicates that about 100 million years ago the ancient Eurasian continent starting from the region where Lhasa is now located, and the South Asian subcontinent where India now lies, were once on two continental plates which lay far apart from one another. Calculations show that the present South Asian subcontinent drifted north at a rate of about six centimeters a year before finally attaching itself to the rest of the Asian continent.

From 1966 to 1968, and again in 1975, stratigraphists and paleontologists in our team recovered from the Permian (about 230 million years ago) layers in southern Tibet, immediately north of the Himalayas, a large quantity of fossil *Glossopteris,* while in the Permo-Carboniferous (270 to 350 million years ago) layers signs of glaciation and fossils of cold-water fauna were found. *Glossopteris* is a genus of seed fern with tongue-shaped fronds which lived in an unvaried cold climate more than 200 million years ago. Up to now, fossils of this genus, known as the Gondwana plant group, have been found only in the South Asian subcontinent, Australia, Africa, the southeastern part of South America, and Antarctica, in geologic layers with glaciers and ice-water sedimentation. The discovery of *Glossopteris* in southern Tibet proves that this area and the South Asian subcontinent belonged originally to the same continental plate, thus definitively advancing the northern limit of the paleogeographic environment, which formerly was known to exist only in the South Asian subcontinent, beyond the Himalayan Range to the southern part of the Qinghai-Tibet Plateau.

By contrast, in the northern part of the Plateau layers of corresponding periods, containing none of the above-mentioned geologic evidence, afforded instead abundant fossils of *Gigantopteris,* a tropical or subtropical genus. It has been found extensively in Carboniferous and Permian layers both in northern and southern China, hence its other name, Cathaysian flora.

6

6. Tourmaline muscovite potash feldspar granite, dating back 10 to 20 million years, is the youngest granite on the Plateau.

7

8

7. Our research team making gravimetric surveys in the Himalayan region.

8. Measuring man-made shock waves is like taking an X-ray picture of the earth. By setting off small explosives about Lake Yamzhog Yumco, and analyzing the variations in the rate of propagation of elastic waves through different kinds of rock layers, we were able to learn about the composition and structure of the Plateau below its surface.

This clearly indicates that about 300 million years ago, with the present-day Yarlung Zangbo as the dividing line, the northern and southern parts of what is now Tibet had totally different climatic conditions and equally distinct forms of life.

From these discoveries the following conclusions can be drawn:

First, that the Plateau is made up of two separate landmasses which once lay some 6,000 kilometers apart. They were joined together in the southern part of the Asian continent and their suture line runs close to the Yarlung Zangbo.

Second, that the northern portion of the Plateau has always been part of the Eurasian continent (also referred to as Laurasia), in the northern hemisphere. Its southern portion, however, was once part of the South Asian subcontinent that includes the Indian peninsula. Originally located in the cold southern part of the southern hemisphere, it was at one time part of a huge continent known as Gondwanaland, which included Australia, Africa, Antarctica, and the southeastern part of South America.

Third, that less than 200 million years ago, Gondwanaland broke up into fragments which subsequently drifted in various directions. The northernmost part moved north across the Equator to merge with the Eurasian continent, thus forming the present-day South Asian subcontinent. The northward movement of this landmass exerted horizontal forces whose pressure caused the elevation of the Qinghai-Tibet Plateau.

Let us have a closer look at the process of the Plateau's upheaval.

Fossil evidence in layers of sedimentary rocks indicates that the Qinghai-Tibet Plateau has a relatively short history of 200 million years, constituting only 5 percent of the earth's history. Before that time the area now occupied by the Plateau was a vast green sea. Here, in the warmer shallows of the northern hemisphere, flourished corals, fusulinids, lamellibranchia, and other invertebrates. Meanwhile, the shallow seas around the northern part of Gondwanaland, later to become the southern part of the Plateau, were still a stretch of frigid waters in the southern hemisphere and yielded little in the way of plant life.

Late in the Triassic period (190 to 225 million years ago), the region covering the Kunlun Mountains and the eastern

Geologic Time Scale and Evolution of Life

Era	Periods and systems	Epochs and series	Million years before present	Evolution of life
Cenozoic	Quaternary	Holocene		Modern man
		Pleistocene		Early man
			2 to 3	
	Tertiary	Pliocene Miocene Oligocene Eocene Paleocene		
			70	Mammalia Angiospermophyta
Mesozoic	Cretaceous		135	
	Jurassic		180	Birds
	Triassic		225	
	Permian		270	Reptiles Gymnospermae
Paleozoic	Carbon-iferous		350	Amphibians
	Devonian		400	
	Silurian		440	Continental Fishes Cryptogamia
	Ordovician		500	
	Cambrian		600	Invertebrates
Proterozoic	Sinian		1000 ?	Algae ?
Archaeozoic	Pre-Sinian		3400 ?	
			4500 ? 6000 ?	
Initial Stage of Development of the Earth				

part of the Jinsha River began to emerge from the sea. Here, in the hot and moist low-lying coastal land, ancient ferns and *Cycadaceae* grew thickly, mixed with tall Ginkgoales and conifers. Then, 50 million years later, in the mid-Jurassic period, both the area north of what is today the Gangdise Mountains and the Hengduan mountain region east of the present Nujiang

River began to rise out of the water. Vegetation differed slightly from that seen earlier on the continent. But the dinosaurs, representative of the vertebrate reptiles, attained unprecedented size for land animals, among them the giant sauropod, which browsed by the shores and in swamps amid trees and reeds.

After another 50 million years, the mid-Cretaceous period, a huge transformation took place. Gondwanaland, far in the southern hemisphere, split into several plates. Hot magma surged up from the asthenosphere to intrude into the widening rifts and then solidified in the fissures. The presence of this rock created horizontal forces which pushed the already separated plates of Gondwanaland farther away from each other. The space between the plates eventually became the Indian Ocean, and the fissures on the continent took the form of deep saddle-shaped trenches between high submarine ridges stretching across the ocean floor.

Of the plates which detached themselves from Gondwanaland, the northernmost one, later to become the South Asian subcontinent, now "floated" north, forcing the denser and thinner oceanic crust of the Tethys Sea north of it to underthrust the thicker but less dense Eurasian continent along the line formed by the present Gar River and the Yarlung. Consequently, the Tethys Sea shrank in area, and the distance between the two continents decreased. This pressure from the south and the continuous remelting of the oceanic crust as it was thrust under the Eurasian continent produced intense agitation within the earth's crust and mantle, which in turn caused faulting in the rock layers to the north, along with violent eruptions and extensive magma intrusion. (The multicolored volcanic and intrusive rocks forming the bulk of the Gangdise Range today were laid down at that time.) As a result, the crust grew steadily thicker and its surface was pushed higher until it finally stood above sea level. This period is referred to as the first phase of the Himalayan upheaval.

On this vast landmass, tall subtropical evergreens and broadleaf trees rose to dominance. The dinosaur, which had reigned supreme in the middle of the Mesozoic era, became extinct and was replaced gradually by mammals capable of controlling their body temperature.

The South Asian subcontinent still pressed northward. It ultimately annexed itself to the Eurasian continent about 40 million years ago, at the beginning of the mid-Eocene epoch of the Cenozoic era, when the lithosphere of the Tethys Sea had gradually melted away in the process of its underthrusting into the Eurasian continent. Because the density and thickness of the two continents were virtually the same, no further underthrusting was possible, so they now met head-on. The tremendous collision compressed the accumulated sedimentary rock layers overlying the ocean floor into complex folds, so that the last remaining denser crustal material at the bottom of the Tethys Sea between the two plates was squeezed up along the line of collision to form a 2,000-kilometer-long ophiolite belt, a type of rock structure composed of ultrabasic rock, basic rock, basic volcanic rock (pillow lava), and radiolarian siliceous rock. This widespread faulting activity was accompanied by another intrusion of magma, and the Gangdise Mountains were thus built up. This was the second phase of the Himalayan movement.

South of the Gangdise Mountains, the climate was mild and humid. Eucalyptus, ficus, and other broadleaf evergreens grew prolifically. These forests were later buried in shallow basins and eventually turned into coal. The climate north of the mountain range was hot and dry, and the waterless inland lakes held only red bed deposits of oxidized ferromagnesian minerals and thin layers of gypsum.

The ridges on the floor of the Indian Ocean continued to spread, but the northward advance of the South Asian subcontinent was greatly arrested by the Eurasian continent. Stress accumulated slowly and imperceptibly on the now fused continent. Then, about 20 million years ago, in the mid-Miocene epoch, the pent-up energy was released. The folded rock layers became more compact. Along the central part of the present Himalayan mountain region, the crust fractured and a huge fault zone more than 2,000 kilometers long appeared, known as the main central fault. Along this fault line and also along the contact plane of various rock layers elsewhere, a series of thrusting and sliding movements occurred during which the older rock layers were pushed up to overlie the younger rock

9

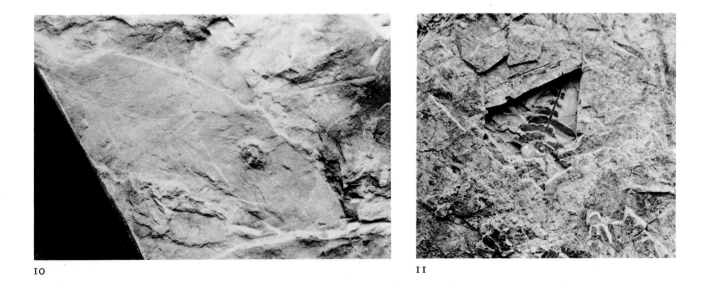

10

11

9. A fossil of the common *Glossopteris*, a seed fern.

10. A fossil of narrow-leaved *Glossopteris*.

11. A *Gigantonoclea* fossil on the surface of a rock layer.

strata. The friction caused by this oversliding led to the remelting of rocks in the crust; magma erupted and set, producing a rock called tourmaline-granite.

Under this tremendous thrusting and compressing, the mighty arc of the Himalayan Range took initial shape. The land north of the range further contracted horizontally in a north-south direction, thus thickening the crust and forcing its surface higher. All this marked the third phase of the building of the Himalayas.

During the Pliocene, the last epoch of the Tertiary period, relatively little tectonic activity took place on the Plateau. In the northern and southern parts of Tibet and in certain ancient lake basins on the south face of the Himalayas, animal fossils show that large herds of mammals such as the *Hipparion* (three-toed horse), *Chilotherium,* giraffe, muntjac, hyena, and gazelle roamed in dense tropical and subtropical forests of palm, bamboo, mountain walnut, and oak, or back and forth between forest and grassland. This indicates that the surface of the Qinghai-Tibet Plateau had not yet attained a very great height. From the geologic position of the Plateau, together with the elevation at which fossils of the *Hipparion* in north China have been found, it can be deduced that the height of the Plateau at that time was about a thousand meters above sea level. Similarly, the Himalayas were not yet high enough to obstruct the migration of these herds of *Hipparion*.

The Pliocene epoch lasted about 9 million years, and toward its end the climate on the Plateau turned cold. Almost 3 million years ago, the Pliocene epoch and with it the Tertiary period ended with violent tectonic movements, and a new period, the Quaternary, was ushered in. During this time the Indian plate thrust down northward along the main boundary fault at the southern foot of the Himalayas. The Plateau, like a gigantic wedge inserted between the rigid Indian peninsula and the Tarim-Alashan landmass (which encompassed the present southern Xinjiang, northern Gansu, and western Inner Mongolia), was pushed up.

Owing to this renewed activity of its older tectonic fissures, the lifting of the Plateau varied greatly from place to place. The Himalayas rose highest, reaching above the snow line, and

12

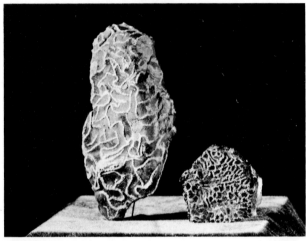

13

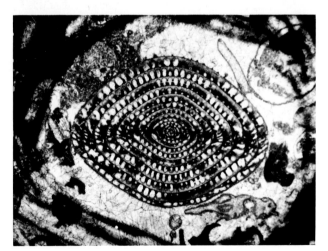

14

12. The fossil *Pecopteris*, found in the vicinity of Shuanghu, northern Tibet.

13. Fossils of the *Catenipora*, a coelenterate animal which lived in the ancient ocean around 500 million years ago.

14. *Fusulina*, protozoans with a shell, which inhabited the ocean bed more than 200 million years ago.

glaciers appeared. Some areas between the mountain ranges subsided along the rift to form relatively deep basins, creating new inland lakes. During the whole Quaternary period, the phenomenal lifting of the Plateau was accompanied by uneven internal vertical movements which absorbed and distributed the stress built up by the persistent spreading of ridges on the bed of the Indian Ocean. This tectonic movement undoubtedly stimulated the magma in the crust and thus induced violent hydrothermal activity on an extensive scale in the southern region of Tibet and continued volcanic activity in its northern part.

Affected by the cyclical changes in climate around the globe, during the Quaternary period the Plateau alternated between hot and cold. It passed through at least three ice ages, during which numerous glaciers formed. The ice ages were interspersed with relatively warmer interglacial periods, and the southern part of Tibet even developed red soils, which indicate a warm climate.

Evidence of human activity dating back at least to the latter period of the Old Stone Age, including primitive stone implements, has been found in the southern part of the Plateau. From the end of the last ice age to about 10,000 years ago, the climate of the Plateau grew warmer. The region was now habitable, and implements belonging to the Middle Stone Age have been discovered in both the southern and northern areas of the Plateau. Finer than their predecessors, their shape and mode of manufacture are similar to those of the same period recovered in the Huanghe (Yellow River) basin.

The Plateau is still rising. Within the last hundred years, four earthquakes exceeding eight on the Richter Scale have occurred on the Plateau and along its perimeter. In 1951, renewed volcanic eruptions took place in the region of the Kunlun Range. Repeated recordings recently made of the water level in the southern part of the Plateau show that this landmass is being elevated at the rate of 3.2 to 12.7 centimeters a year.

15

16

17

15. Fossil rib of a sauropod, measuring 1.5 meters long.

16. Fossil teeth of a sauropod.

17. Pebble-bearing slate of glaciomarine conglomerate, formed in the late Carboniferous period. This piece of Gondwana sediment was carried north along with the Indian plate to the northern slopes of the Himalayas.

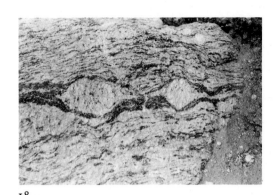

18

19

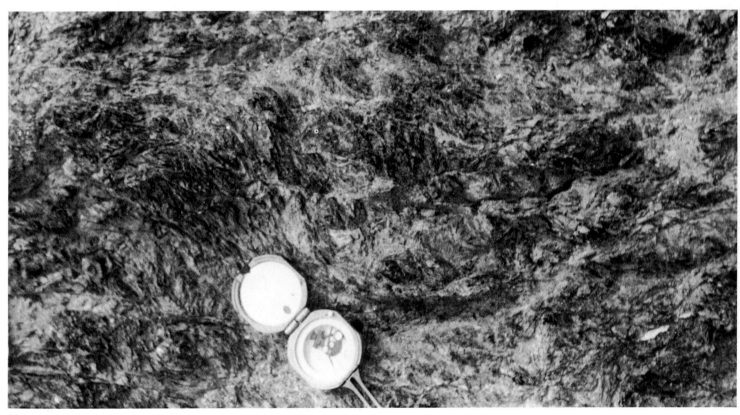

20

18. Ocular gneiss, an ancient metamorphic rock that forms the base of the Himalayas. Owing to the rising of the mountains, this rock now appears on slopes at high altitudes.

19. Ridged layers of the Cretaceous period, with intricate drag folds and cleavage planes, found in Xigaze in southern Tibet. Their axial surface slopes south, indicating that they had been formed by the tremendous horizontal pressure applied during the collision of the Indian and Eurasian plates.

The Yarlung Zangbo
Ophiolite Group:
Illustrations 20–25

20. Ophiolite. The ultrabasic rock of the upper mantle is often ophiolitized. The rock is very fragmented, schistosized and mylonitized. An ophiolitic group is composed of rocks which, after weathering, show a serpentine, dominantly dark-green pattern.

21

22

23

21. Ophiolite melange rock, consisting of basic rock (lighter color) surrounded by heavily schistosized ultrabasic rock. These were mixed and compressed by violent tectonic action.

22. This peculiar structure, given the name of pillow lava, was formed by a volcanic eruption at the bottom of the Tethys Sea. It is usually dark red.

23. This radiolarian siliceous rock, formed of deep-sea sediments, was pushed up along with other rock of the ophiolite group during the upheaval of the Himalayas. Siliceous rock is usually whitish.

24

25

24. Allochthonous rock, an exotic block transported from the faraway south and left on the southern side of the ophiolite zone after the collision of the Indian and the Eurasian plates. The white section is Permian limestone and below it is Triassic arenaceous shale.

25. This is a complex accumulation of Cretaceous flysch, another type of exotic block, whose periphery is often fragmental and contorted. Its particles could have been deposited by water running down during the violent tectonic movements in the past.

26

27

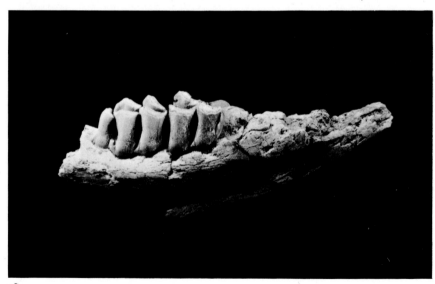

28

26. Fossil of lower jaw of a *Hipparion*.

27. Lower jaw of a *Chilotherium*.

28. Lower jaw of a giraffe.

29

30

29. A landslide.

30. The Qinghai-Tibet Plateau is still rising. The latest tectonic movement caused a series of east-west normal faults (depressions) in the lake sediments formed 2 million years ago.

3
FROZEN WONDERLAND

The overwhelming size and complex forms of the glaciers of Tibet and their accompanying phenomena make the Qinghai-Tibet Plateau a magnificent world of ice. The Qinghai-Tibet Plateau is the most developed region of modern glaciers to be found in the middle to lower latitudes of the globe. The Nyainqentanglha Range, to the north of the middle section of the Yarlung Zangbo valley, has more than 5,000 square kilometers of glaciers alone, which exceeds by far the glacial area of the European Alps. The Rongbuk and Kongbu glaciers on Mount Qomolangma, and the Yeborkangjle glacier to the north of Mount Xixabangma are all of considerable size. Ice pinnacles, ice caverns, and dazzling glacier lakes are unique landscapes of the Plateau's glacial areas. The ice pinnacles here are far more spectacular than the snow dunes of the Andes of South America. Whereas the latter are formed by melting névé snow (the partially compacted granular surface layer) and last only one to two years, the former are shaped from glacial ice by the intense sunshine of the area and may remain standing for as long as a century.

It may seem surprising that glaciers lie at such low latitudes, for the Plateau is about on a level with the lower Mississippi River or North Africa. The explanation lies in the topography of the area, created by the violent lifting up of the Plateau, and the intensely cold climate resulting from the tremendous elevation. Many mountains here are above the snow line, the line above which solid precipitation such as snow and hail accumulates from year to year. Glaciers occur exclusively in mountainous regions above the snow line. Mountains below the snow line only carry seasonal snow. The snow line of Mount Qomolangma is approximately 5,800 to 6,000 meters above sea level, but the mountain rises 3,000 meters above the snow line, where snow accumulates and glaciers originate. Constant avalanches of snow from the slopes feed the upper reaches of the glaciers, so that the surface layers of ice and snow grow increasingly thicker. Under this weight, the glaciers begin to slide, entering the valleys like tongues of moving ice. That part of the glacier below the snow line is where the ice melts and evaporates (the ablation zone). Because ablation and intake of ice at the glacial tongue are generally in equilibrium, the

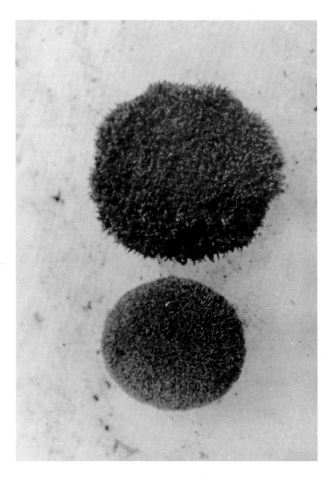

1. Alpine moss (*Tortula*) grows 2,500 to 4,200 meters above sea level on glaciers in southeastern Tibet. It clings to bits of soil or glacier sediment, and, being constantly rolled about by the moving glacier and the surface meltwater, grows in all directions and becomes ball-shaped.

positions of the termini of the glaciers are fairly constant. Glaciers begin as solid precipitation and turn into meltwater as they approach their termini.

If the formation of glaciers on the Qinghai-Tibet Plateau depends upon the high altitude of the terrain, then the amount of snow that falls determines to a large extent the character of the glacier. An analysis of rainfall data developed by the expedition in various parts of the Plateau showed that the Himalayas are in effect a huge barrier that arrests the wet monsoons of the Indian Ocean from the south, leaving the interior of the Plateau extremely cold and dry and snow accumulation on the glaciers very scant. The water equivalent of the annual snowfall here is generally only 500 to 800 millimeters. Such a thin layer of snow melts rapidly in the summer. In such circumstances, it is only in very high altitudes, where the temperature is very low, that perennial snow can stay and glaciers appear. Consequently, the snow line is normally high in the cold and dry interior of the Plateau.

The snow line on the northern slopes of the Himalayas and the Ngari Prefecture in western Tibet reaches 6,200 meters, the highest yet found in the northern hemisphere. The glaciers here exist only because of the extremely low temperatures. They are therefore referred to as cold or continental glaciers.

In sharp contrast, snow falls in abundance in the vicinity of the bend of the Yarlung Zangbo in the southeastern part of Tibet, owing to the influence of the Indian Ocean's monsoons. The annual layer of névé snow in this part of the Plateau often reaches 2,000 to 3,000 millimeters in water equivalent. This substantially lowers the snow line. In the Bomi-Zayu area in southeastern Tibet, the snow line is frequently between 4,500 to 4,800 meters, more than 1,000 meters lower than in the Qomolangma region. Although the mountains here attain an elevation of only 6,000 meters above sea level, their peaks rise sufficiently above the snow line for glaciers of immense proportions to form. The Qiaqing glacier, for example, on the southern slopes of the Nyainqentanglha Range northwest of Lake Yiong, is 33 kilometers in length and about 172 square kilometers in area, making it a major glacier on the Plateau.

2. The boulders carried along by the glacier grind against each other, leaving glacial striations behind. Typically these are arc-shaped, because the flow of a glacier is much slower than that of a river.

54

The ice covering this region is formed at a temperature not far below its melting point, so we describe the glaciers as temperate or maritime. Owing to the higher temperature of the ice, its pronounced plasticity, and its larger volume, the velocity of these glaciers is greater than that of the continental type. Whereas the flow of continental glaciers generally does not exceed 100 meters a year, temperate glaciers in southeastern Tibet have been recorded as moving at a rate of 300 to 400 meters a year.

At present, the maritime glacier standing at the lowest altitude is the Abzha glacier of Zayu in southeastern Tibet, whose terminus ends 2,400 meters above sea level. The mean annual temperature here reaches 11° C, making this a montane subtropical forest zone where corn, tea, bamboo, and similar vegetation flourishes. On the maritime glaciers there thrives a varied community of organisms, including snow-algae, mosses, ice worms, and springtails. These denizens of the glaciers have developed their own natural defenses to withstand the cold.

The glaciers of the Qinghai-Tibet Plateau act as reservoirs of frozen water. They are the fountainheads of several large rivers: the mighty Changjiang (Yangtze) emerges from the Jianggen Dirunan glacier of snowcapped Mount Geladandong, and the Yarlung Zangbo has its source in the Jiemayangzong glacier. With the advent of summer, the glaciers "turn on their taps," releasing meltwater to swell the rivers and streams. The roaring torrents of ice and meltwater converge to form the Changjiang, Huanghe (Yellow), Indus, and Ganges—all of which have nourished civilizations of the East since antiquity.

3

3. In summer the glaciers melt at different rates. The meltwaters converge in the lower areas to form glacial lakes. Shoots of ice stand in the water, in which plankton is found.

4. Melting ice at the terminus of the Amugang glacier.

6

5. The Western Rongbuk glacier below Mount Qomolangma (Everest).

6. Ice pinnacles at the terminus of the Central Rongbuk glacier. The Plateau's dry climate, coupled with intense solar radiation, causes the glacier's uneven surfaces to thaw in varying degrees and form these ice pinnacles, or seracs.

7. En route through a forest of seracs.

7

8

9

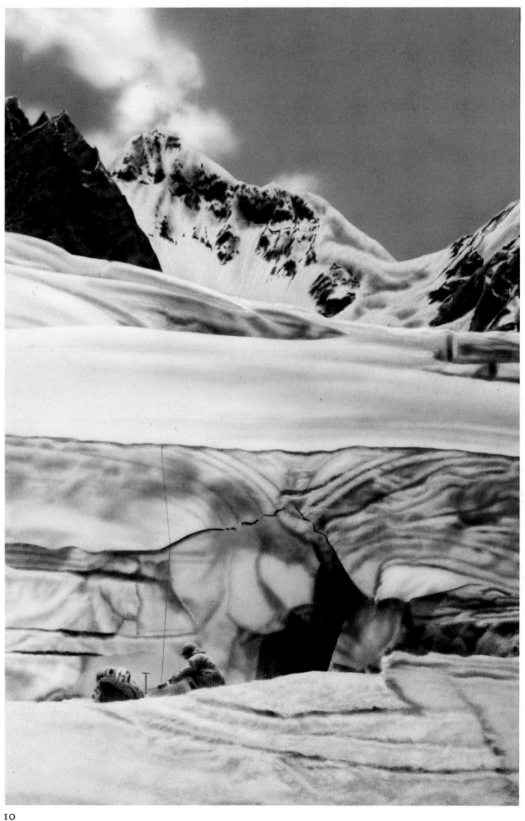

10

8. The Amugang glacier on the southern slopes of Mount Muztag, highest peak of the Kunlun Range, is a typical continental glacier. Its lowest point is 5,480 meters above sea level.

9. The middle section of the Abzha glacier, a typical maritime glacier, penetrates a mixed conifer and broadleaf forest at 2,400 meters above sea level.

10. Annual layers of granular snow in the névé basin form a chronological record of the glacier's development.

11

11. Glacier meltwaters cut deep into the crevasses of the glacier and flow as streams which carve out fantastic valleys of ice.

12. The rate of ablation in maritime glaciers is high, varying from 5 to 10 centimeters each day. Here we see a rapidly melting ice surface.

13

13. The névé basin at the head of the Abzha glacier. It is fed by avalanches of accumulated snow from the surrounding slopes. The snow turns to ice and, pushed by its own weight, spills out of the basin and moves down the slopes to become a glacier.

14

14. A view of the Zhuxigou glacier, fed directly by avalanches, and thus known as a snow-avalanche glacier.

15

15. This glacial tongue has reached the edge of a precipice. Falling as glacier avalanches, the ice collects below and, if it accumulates, becomes another glacier. This type is known as a suspended glacier.

16. The velocity of a maritime glacier increases at the section where the glaciated valley slopes sharply, to form a glacier cascade.

17

17. Rocks at the bottom of the moving glacier cut down into the bedrock. In some places the exposed bedrock, shaped by glacier overriding, resembles the backs of a flock of sheep and hence is given the name "sheepback rocks," or *roches moutonnées*.

18. Karila glacier is on a peak 6,500 meters ➤ above sea level in southern Tibet. It has advanced twice, once 3,000 years ago and again in the nineteenth century. The present retreat of the glacier shows that the climate on the Plateau in recent times has become warmer and drier.

4 GEYSERS, SPOUTERS, FUMAROLES

Between the Himalayas and the Gangdise-Nyainqentanglhas, extending for 2,000 kilometers from the Sengge River valley in the west to the fringe of the Hengduan Mountains in the east, lies a remarkable strip of territory unlike any other in China. Formed as a consequence of the great Himalayan mountain-making movement that began 70 million years ago, it is known as the Himalayan geothermal belt. A geothermal belt is a strip of territory in which the internal heat of the earth is conducted to the surface and released aboveground through the action of volcanoes, geysers, boiling springs, and similar phenomena.

The presence of a strip of this kind in this part of China has long been suspected by geologists. Such a belt extends west of the Qinghai-Tibet Plateau through Iran, Turkey, Greece, and Italy. Another reaches east of the Plateau, running through Yunnan Province in China and south through Burma to Malaysia, where it joins the great geothermal belt that rings the Pacific Ocean. It was only logical to think that there must be a link between the Mediterranean belt and the Yunnan–Burma belt. All it would take to connect the two would be a relatively short strip running across Tibet.

Evidence of geothermal activities on the Qinghai-Tibet Plateau has existed since the end of the nineteenth century. Reports of a few western investigators tell of volcanoes in North Tibet and hot springs in South Tibet. But there was no thorough scientific study of the area until 1973, when the Chinese Academy of Sciences launched its research program. Between 1973 and 1976, teams of scientists made four expeditions to different parts of the Plateau, spending six months in each, questioning the local inhabitants and exploring the region in an attempt to confirm the existence of geothermal activity.

Our research was amply rewarded. While we discovered no volcanoes in southern Tibet—a puzzling fact not yet fully explained—we found no fewer than 600 areas in which heat from deep inside the earth's crust is diffused aboveground in the form of hot water or steam. This is the greatest concentration of active hydrothermal districts yet found in China. It includes every known type of hydrothermal activity: hot springs and pools, boiling spouters, boiling springs, fumaroles (crevices through which hot gases are released), geysers, and hydrothermal explosions. These last two are rare geologic phenomena of great scientific and potential economic value, and they occur in only a very few places in the world. "Old Faithful" in Yellowstone Park is the most famous geyser, and only the United States, New Zealand, and China have all the phenomena listed. Iceland has all but the thermal explosions. Generally, geyser eruptions must measure 3 meters (almost 10 feet) in height to be counted.

There are three geyser districts in Tibet, all of them located in the valley under the southern slopes of the Gangdise-Nyainqentanglhas. The Takejia geyser district of Ngamring County, with four vents, is the largest. The survey team members who visited the district in July 1975 enjoyed a spectacular sight. The geyser is at the foot of a snowcapped mountain that rises 6,000 meters above sea level in the middle of the Gangdise Range. As we watched in this dramatic setting, a jet of water and steam, about 2 meters in diameter, suddenly burst from the ground before us amid thunderous roars and shot up to a height of some 20 meters, white vapor rising above it for another 40 to 50 meters. This was followed by sheets of hot rain, which fell on those of us who were not quick enough to get out of range. Then a rainbow appeared. Before we had time to marvel at the sight, the water and steam shrank back gradually until both disappeared. Silence prevailed once more.

Geysers are known for their sudden eruptions, great momentum, and alternating periods of ejection and quiescence. They are generally found in so-called sinter terraces, which have been formed by the accumulation of silica deposits from the hot water. (An enormous amount of silica is present in the water of certain high-temperature springs. As the water evaporates and cools off, the silica forms sinter, some of which may eventually change into agate.) The geyser's action is produced by a kind of boiler system beneath the terrace. The principal part of the system is an underground reservoir into which water seeps through crevices in the walls. Through passages that are in communication with heat sources deep in the earth's crust, hot water and steam are transferred into the reservoir, which is

1. Although the Kau hydrothermal district is 4,400 meters above sea level, it is infested with an astonishing number of snakes, living proof that the Plateau was once at a much lower elevation. Only the warmth from the geysers and fumaroles enables them to survive in the area's present freezing climate.

connected to the vent aboveground by a duct. When the water accumulated in the reservoir reaches the boiling point and expands into steam, pressure in the reservoir exceeds the atmospheric pressure in the duct. Thus the water is forced to the surface, and the geyser erupts until the reservoir is empty. Then all becomes quiet again. The infiltration of more hot water into the reservoir starts the process all over again.

A hydrothermal explosion is an even rarer and more violent phenomenon. It occurs when hot subterranean water, lying relatively close to the earth's surface, is converted into steam by a sudden increase in heat, owing to movements of the magma in the depths of the earth or to a seismic shock. The steam erupts through the ground into the air with enormous force, carrying with it mud, sand, and rocks.

There are ten known explosion districts in the Himalayan geothermal belt. Unlike geysers, explosions do not occur at a relatively fixed place or time, and in any given district they vary in frequency. They may occur as often as a dozen times a year or as seldom as once in several decades. Since their pattern is unpredictable, and since few people live near the districts in question, hydrothermal explosions are not often observed. One that was observed occurred on November 12, 1975, in the Qupu hydrothermal district on the southeastern bank of Lake Mapam Yumco. Some eyewitnesses, who were standing on the far side of the Za River several hundred meters away, told members of our expedition what they had seen. They heard a terrifying boom and saw cattle and sheep grazing in the area scatter in all directions, while Qupu was wrapped in billowing fumes. A column of black vapor shot 800 or 900 meters into the air, turned into a bank of black clouds, and drifted away; then rocks fell to the ground, some landing at the very feet of the onlookers.

The craters created by hydrothermal explosions bear mute witness to the awesome events that have taken place. In the initial period after the explosion, the crater has the shape of an inverted bell—wider at the mouth than at the base. It is filled with boiling water, which, cooling with the passage of time, eventually becomes a warm-water pool or lake. Some of these bodies of water are very large. In the Qupu hydrothermal

2

3

2. The water from a hot spring in the Hengduan Mountains has a very high salt content. The local people dry the spring water in the sun to obtain salt.

3. Liquid steam—a mixture of hot water and steam—erupting from a well drilled in the Yangbajain hydrothermal district near Lhasa. The first liquid-steam geothermal power station in China began operating in October 1979.

district, we saw a warm-water crater 100 meters in diameter at the orifice, surrounded by 12-meter-high banks of mud and sand that had been thrown up by the explosion—one which must have been far greater than the one witnessed in 1975. Nearby were many smaller hot-water pools, sparkling like sapphires in their settings of white siliceous sinter. In some, the surface of the water was as smooth as a mirror, while in others it seethed incessantly. The slightest breeze wafted vapor all around, screening the pools behind mists of steam.

In the Yangbajain thermal field of Lhasa, we visited a hot-water lake with an area of 7,350 square meters and an average temperature of 50° C. On sunny, windless mornings, a huge column of white vapor floats up from the azure waters to the azure sky, against the distant background of the magnificent Nyainqentanglha Mountains. The imaginative Tibetan people call this large hot-water lake the tea caldron of the mountain god of Nyainqentanglha (the Tibetans brew their tea in great quantities).

When a high-temperature pool is in a later stage of development, the hot water overflowing the orifice evaporates quickly in the dry climate and intense sunshine, leaving layers of mineral deposits around the vent. (Sulphur is obtainable from hot water and vapor in many of the high-temperature districts in Kau.) This constant action thickens the sinter terrace, reducing the likelihood of another explosion. Moreover, our research team found that in certain pools the deposits accumulate more rapidly around the rim of the opening than around the pool walls, so that the top gradually closes in like the mouth of a jar. This suggests that the water-filled crater may eventually develop into the type of underground reservoir found in geysers. The research team concluded that an explosion represents the early stage of a high-temperature hydrothermal action, while a geyser signifies a matured stage of that action—the two phenomena are closely related.

We saw many other striking manifestations of hydrothermal activity in the Himalayan geothermal belt. The boiling spouters of Namling County, for example, emit endless jets of water and steam; the Rugyog fumarole of Saga County sends up vapors and gases as scorching as the breath of a furnace; the Burong boiling spring district of Damxung County has dozens of vents with constantly seething water.

These vigorous hydrothermal activities, which would seem to be of only scientific interest, suggest the practical possibility of exploiting terrestrial heat as a new source of energy. The Himalayan geothermal belt provides Tibet with ample supplies of thermal energy, and some of these are already being put to use. The water from the Qabka hot spring in the vicinity of Xaitongmoin County, for example, is channeled for use in greenhouses, bathhouses, and swimming pools. The Yangbajain hydrothermal field northwest of Lhasa, an area of 20 square kilometers, offers even greater possibilities, diffusing into the atmosphere 110,000 kilocalories of heat per second, amounting annually to the calorific value of 470,000 tons of standard-grade coal. The area is now being developed.

The Himalayan geothermal belt also holds precious mineral resources. The superheated waters of the area contain large quantities of certain valuable elements that are rare in other parts of the world. For example, one of the boiling springs in South Tibet represents a rich supply of cesium. The most highly electropositive element known, cesium is widely used in the cinema, television, and national defense industries, and some scientists regard it as one of the most promising metals for use in space exploration and the exploitation of solar energy.

In addition to this important metal, the hot water of the hydrothermal districts contains high concentrations of boron, lithium, rubidium, arsenic, and fluorine. These elements are significant not only as mineral resources but also as keys to the understanding of certain puzzling geologic phenomena. For instance, similar combinations of elements are found in certain North Tibet salt lakes, in areas where many ancient sinters are discernible. This suggests that the salinity of the lakes is the result of previous hydrothermal activities in the region.

The activities visible on the surface of the Himalayan geothermal belt bear witness to the mysterious agitation far below. Study of these activities will throw light on movements hidden in the depths of the earth and on the geologic history of the most prodigious plateau in the world.

4

5

6

7

4. A typical small-explosion crater in the Kurme hydrothermal district south of the Yarlung Zangbo. A dozen explosions occur here every year.

5. A jar-shaped hot-water pool in the Buxiunglanggu hydrothermal district south of the Yarlung Zangbo.

6. A fumarole on an islet midstream in the Yangbajain River. When the river floods, the vent is inundated.

7. The Kau hydrothermal district south of the Yarlung Zangbo. The main vent of the geyser is spouting boiling water and steam more than a meter into the air.

8

8. The principal vent of the Takejia geyser, at the foot of the southern slopes of the Gangdise Range. The Takejia geyser district has four vents, two of which are the largest discovered so far in China.

9. Close-up of the Takejia geyser's principal vent.

10. An eruption of the principal vent of the Takejia geyser, as seen by the research team. A column of water and steam 2 meters in diameter shoots some 20 meters into the air, while steam on top of the column rises another 40 to 50 meters. Eruptions from the vent are irregular, varying in both height and frequency.

9

11

11. An impressive hot-water lake, 16.1 meters deep and 7,350 square meters in area, in the Yangbajain hydrothermal district. The water from this lake, whose temperature varies between 45° and 57°C, flows into a tributary of the Yarlung Zangbo, at a rate of 24 liters per second.

12. Layers of calcareous sinter formed by ▶ calcium carbonate deposited by a hot spring in the Tajie hydrothermal district.

13

14

13. A large-scale hydrothermal explosion occurred on the evening of November 12, 1975, in Qupu, southeast of Lake Mapam Yumco. According to the reports of eye-witnesses, a column of black vapor spouted 800 to 900 meters into the air. Now the crater, with a 25-meter orifice, seethes with boiling water.

14. The Capu geyser, also at the foot of the southern slopes of the Gangdise Mountains. Eruptions from the principal vent, reaching a height of 7 meters, are regular and frequent, occurring 208 times every twenty-four hours.

15. In the Bibilong hydrothermal district, three boiling spouters issue from the granite. As superheated water rises close to the surface, the drop in pressure causes it to boil. A mixture of water and steam erupts from crevices in the rock in a perpetual stream.

16. A forest of sinter pillars in the Lungmar hydrothermal district on the North Tibet plateau. Such formations occur only at high altitudes, where solar radiation is strong, and in an arid climate. Under these conditions the water ejected by a hot spring evaporates very quickly, and the accumulation of mineral deposits around its orifice builds higher and higher, forming a kind of hollow pillar. When at last the the passage becomes blocked so that the jet of water can no longer force its way out, the spring seeks another weak point in the earth's surface for a vent, and the process is repeated.

17

17. This crater in Qupu is 80 meters in diameter at its bottom and 100 meters at its orifice. Although no one witnessed the explosion, the size of the crater reveals that it must have been even greater than the one that occurred in November 1975.

18

18. A hot spring on an elevated sinter terrace in the Qulung hydrothermal district. The water spills down over a beautiful, steep sinter cone.

5
MIGHTY QOMOLANGMA (MOUNT EVEREST)

In the middle of the great arc formed by the Himalayas, some of the loftiest mountain peaks in the world rise in a shroud of mist, seeming to compete in height and magnificence. Here, standing proudly among snowcapped pinnacles, is the highest mountain on earth. Westerners know it as Mount Everest, but for centuries the people of Tibet have called it by the name of their most beautiful goddess: Qomolangma.

Chinese scientists have measured the height of Mount Qomolangma as 8,848.13 meters above sea level. But the thick layers of limestone of which the mountain is composed, and which now reach so spectacularly into the sky, were originally formed at the bottom of the sea. They were laid down about 450 million years ago, in the Ordovician period of the early Palaeozoic era. The history of these layers can be traced, because each succeeding geologic period has left its mark in the sedimentary layers.

Thirty million years ago the sea bottom that was to become the Himalayas began to be pushed up, and this movement is

1. On May 17, 1975, Chinese mountaineers set up a surveying marker on the top of Mount Qomolangma. The summit was found to be 10 meters long and one meter wide. At left, the marker on the summit. At right, members of the research mission take measurements from a point several miles from the summit. They calculated the present height of Qomolangma to be 8,848.13 meters above the average level of the Yellow Sea, as established by the Qingdao Tide Observation Center.

still in progress. Qomolangma continues to rise along with the rest of the range, and were it not for the constant erosion that simultaneously wears it down, its summit would now be nearly 20,000 meters above sea level.

North of Mount Qomolangma is North Peak, 7,580 meters in elevation. The two mountains are linked together by the famous North Col, a saddle-shaped depression in the ridgeline, known to mountaineers as a formidable barrier. At the lowest part of the saddle is a sheer wall of dark green ice, 400 meters high and crisscrossed by deep crevasses. Climbers seek routes up through the crevasses, but at any point huge chunks of ice, some as heavy as a hundred tons, may split off from the steep slopes and come crashing down, often causing a chain reaction. The swift falls of ice and snow that may take place at any moment are a tremendous hazard to climbers. It was here in 1922 that seven Sherpas, members of a British team, were engulfed by an avalanche. In 1975, three scientists from our Chinese research mission, together with a team of professional mountaineers, successfully ascended the ice wall of the North Col, bringing back valuable scientific data and achieving a world record for mountaineering by scientists.

Below the North Col lies a deep, wide, crescent-shaped basin. Enormous amounts of snow from avalanches have accumulated in this gigantic hollow. Under the intense sunshine, the surface snow melts and runs down into the crevasses. The water seeps into the interstices of the granular snow and, freezing again, cements the individual grains into solid ice. Pressed by the tremendous weight of successive layers of ice, the hardened mass slides down the slope to the edge of the basin, forming the source of the Central Rongbuk glacier. Stretching north of the basin for 15 kilometers, the Central Rongbuk is swelled by the East and West Rongbuks and more than thirty other glaciers, which feed into it like the tributaries of a river. The whole system covers some 200 square kilometers.

Because of variations in the terrain, in the degree of friction, and in the amount of ice flowing in from the various tributaries, different parts of a glacier move at different speeds. All along its course, masses of ice change their shapes. Elevations and depressions appear on the surface, and the uneven intensity of sunshine they receive produces different degrees of melting. These conditions lead to the formation of a forest of ice towers, or seracs, at the lower end of the glacier. These jagged crystal pinnacles, along with the other magnificent creations—curtains of icicles; walls of ice; tables of ice; mounds, caves, and lakes of ice—are all the work of the master sculptor, the sun.

This glittering, fantastic landscape is as beautiful as any on earth, but as alien as any on the moon. Man, the intruder, assaulting the heights of Qomolangma, can survive only with the help of modern technology, overcoming for a brief time the three deadly factors of cold, wind, and rarefied air.

The most overwhelming aspect of the environment is the cold. In January, the coldest month of the year, the average temperature at an altitude equal to that of the summit of Mount Qomolangma is about $-36°$ C, and it may drop to an extreme of $-60°$ C. Even in the warmest month, July, the average temperature is $-19°$ C, and at no time of the year does it rise above freezing. At these polar temperatures, if a man's skin touches metal, it will stick and peel off. But because Qomolangma is located near the Tropic of Cancer, and because the sun has to penetrate an atmosphere only one-third as dense as that at sea level, its rays are very strong. Thus at noontime around the summer solstice, a climber experiences a curious anomaly: standing facing the sun, he feels an arctic wind at his back and genial warmth in front, as one does at an ordinary altitude when facing a campfire on a cold day. The intense solar radiation that brings welcome warmth, however, is in itself a hazard. To a climber without sunglasses, the strong ultraviolet rays and the dazzling reflections from snow and ice present the constant danger of red and swollen eyes, unbearable pain, and even snow blindness.

As for the wind, the second great difficulty with which mountaineers and scientists have to contend, only in the month of October, and again from March to May, is the weather calm enough for climbing. From June to September, the Qomolangma region is under the influence of the monsoons that blow in from the Indian Ocean. The mountaintops are lost in seas of clouds, and violent snowstorms are frequent. From November to February, the global southwest jet stream moves in from the north, battering the summit with winds of hurricane force that may reach a velocity of 87 meters per second. A climber facing winds of this speed would be subject to 100 kilograms of pressure. Even in the summer climbing season, strong winds may suddenly arise. When a storm comes up, often whirling not only snow and ice but also sand and stones, the ambitious climber faces unimaginable hardships and the greatest danger.

Professional mountaineers, aware of the invisible enemy that may lie in wait for them at higher altitudes, have learned to judge its movements by the "flag cloud." In winter and spring, when the prevailing west wind meets the peak of Qomolangma, it divides around the summit, pushing ahead of it the moisture-laden air that has risen from the southern slopes of the Himalayas. In the calm air on the sheltered east face of the mountain, this moisture condenses into a white, pennant-shaped cloud, pointed east. When the wind is around Force 9 (about 50 m.p.h.) at the summit, the flag cloud is at a right angle to the peak. When the wind is weaker, the cloud tilts up, and when it gains momentum, the flag tilts down. Mountaineers keep an anxious watch on this natural weather vane and determine their climbing program in accordance with its dictates.

But the greatest enemy of the men and women who seek to conquer Qomolangma is the rarefied air. At 3,000 meters above sea level, human beings generally begin to have physiological reactions to the reduced supply of oxygen: breathing is accelerated and heavy, and blood circulation speeds up. These automatic reactions enable the body to maintain normal functions, but they also have certain adverse effects. The increased respiration entails an increase in the amount of carbon dioxide breathed out, and this creates an imbalance between the acid and alkali in the respiratory system. The relative excess of alkali may result in dizziness, nausea, and even vomiting. Accelerated circulation, meanwhile, means a more rapid heartbeat and an increase of blood in certain organs. This is especially noticeable in the extracranial vessels, where the increased volume of blood causes great pressure, producing throbbing headaches. The lack of oxygen also causes dysfunction of the stomach and intestines, resulting in loss of appetite, and disrupts metabolism, producing an excess reserve of lactic and acetone acids in the muscles, so that the climber feels enormous fatigue. These symptoms are collectively known as "mountain sickness."

At an elevation of 5,000 meters, the air contains only about half as much oxygen as at sea level. At 7,000 meters, the height of the North Col, the amount of oxygen is reduced to the minimum requirement for man, and this is known as the "dangerous altitude." At 8,000 meters, still below the summit of Mount Qomolangma, the oxygen supply is only one-third of that at sea level. This altitude is called the "death line."

Nevertheless, healthy persons can become acclimatized to the rarefied air through step-by-step adaptation. For example, most of the members of our scientific mission of 1975 came from low-altitude areas, yet we were able to work for several months at our base camp, between 5,000 and 6,000 meters

2. The Rongbuk Lamasery, 5,000 meters above sea level. This was the highest community in the world until the 1950s, when maintenance workers on the Qinghai-Tibet and Sichuan-Tibet highways established permanent camps at still higher elevations.

above sea level. During our first attempt to reach the summit of Qomolangma, some members of the team were caught in bad weather at 8,600 meters. We struggled for three days and two nights, consuming as little of the oxygen we carried with us as possible. One mountaineer, a Tibetan woman, adapted so well to the rarefied atmosphere that she was able to move about, cooking and caring for the victims of mountain sickness, without using any oxygen from her tank.

When nine members of the team finally had the summit under their feet, they stayed there for an hour and ten minutes. They set up a red marker for surveyors waiting on the lower slopes, collected rock specimens, shot film, and, in accordance with mountain-climbing tradition, planted our national flag.

Since the first, historic ascent of Qomolangma in 1953 by Tenzing of Nepal and Hillary of New Zealand, the summit has been attained nineteen times, by mountaineers from sixteen countries. The goal of these climbers—and of those, no less to be honored, who have failed or lost their lives in the attempt—was to reach the highest point on earth. Their successes are hailed as national triumphs. Our Chinese research team of 1975 had a different purpose, however. It was composed not of mountaineers but of geologists, geophysicists, meteorologists, botanists, biologists, and physiologists. Our aim was not merely to reach the peak but to study the environment and man's adaptation to it. Science knows no national boundaries, and in this sense, our expedition to Mount Qomolangma represents an advance in the struggle of all mankind to understand and conquer nature.

4

3. Mount Qomolangma, the crown of the earth, rises above the clouds, dominating a chain of peaks on the Sino-Nepalese border.

4. Collecting rock specimens on the North Col.

6

◄ 5. Approaching the North Col. The 400-meter wall of ice and snow is visible at the upper right. In the foreground is the crescent-shaped névé basin, the source of the East Rongbuk glacier.

6. Mount Qomolangma is snowcapped all year round and constantly shrouded in mist.

7. Camping in a world of ice and snow.

8

9

8. The magnificent mountain appears between ice pinnacles of the Rongbuk glacier.

9. This glittering ice cave stands at the terminus of the Rongbuk glacier, where the climate is warmer than at higher elevations. At one time a river of meltwater ran under the glacier, forming a tunnel in the ice. The roof of the tunnel at last thawed and collapsed at this point, creating an entrance to the crystal palace beneath.

10

11

10. An ice mushroom on the Rongbuk glacier. These forms are often found at a glacier's terminus. Protected by a large slab of fluvioglacial drift, the ice beneath it does not melt as quickly as that around it in the intense sunshine of the Plateau, causing the mushroom to form.

11. In the forest of seracs near the end of the Rongbuk glacier. Some of these ice formations are 40 to 50 meters high, while others are less than half a meter in height. Seracs are created by uneven melting under the intense solar radiation of the warmer season.

6

YARLUNG ZANGBO— THE GREAT RIVER

The Yarlung is the highest river in the world. It crosses the southern part of the Qinghai–Tibet Plateau at an average altitude of 4,000 meters above sea level. For this reason, it was formerly referred to by the Tibetans as the Yangqiao Zangbo, meaning "water that flows from the highest peak." Its length of 2,057 kilometers makes it the sixth longest river in China, and its mean annual flow of 4,500 cubic meters per second, which exceeds that of the Huanghe (Yellow), places it third in velocity. This prodigious flow of water, aided by the sheer drop afforded by the topography of the Plateau, promises a hydroelectric potential of 100 million kilowatts, which would put it second in China only to the Changjiang (Yangtze), and on a par with the Congo River in Africa. The Yarlung is also a well-known international waterway. On entering northeast India, it becomes the Brahmaputra, which eventually discharges into the Bay of Bengal in the Indian Ocean.

Geologic evidence indicates that the Yarlung is a relatively young river which has formed only in the last few million years. Fed by the Jiemayangzong River to the north and the Kubi River to the southwest, it emerges from the northern slopes of the Himalayan Range as the Damqog, or Maquan, River. Formerly, some explorers believed that the Kubi was the main headspring of the Yarlung, because its volume was judged to be larger. Others held that the Yarlung's true source was the Jiemayangzong, because its course was longer, a belief shared by the Tibetans. Our research team determined that the Jiemayangzong is indeed longer than the Kubi by 24 kilometers and that its drainage basin is about twice as large. Furthermore, in August 1975, we established that the volume is in fact about twice that of the Kubi River. This proves conclusively that the Jiemayangzong is the true source of the Yarlung Zangbo.

Southwest of the Jiemayangzong River towers a snowcapped peak, 6,562.7 meters above sea level. On its eastern slope, in a broad U-shaped trough, lies the Jiemayangzong glacier. As this huge mass of ice emerges from the valley, its progress is obstructed by a ridge in the form of a horse's head, which splits the glacier into two. The horse's snout is a huge 10-meter-tall fluvioglacial drift (a mass deposited by the glacier), on the top of the ridge, and its ears are two glacial extensions protruding

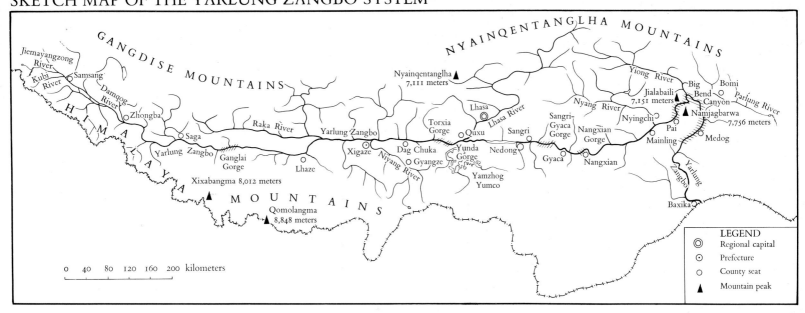

from the glacial valley. This entire area lies 5,200 meters above sea level. With the advent of spring, as the sun blazes down, rivulets of meltwater appear on the glacier's surface or issue from beneath the glacial tongues, silently declaring the birth of the mighty Yarlung Zangbo.

Strands of meltwater from the nearby glaciers flow down to the Jiemayangzong River, which forms branching waterways on the moraine-laden former glacial bed, where deposits of lateral and terminal moraines from the retreated glacier block the meltwater, creating moraine lakes of various sizes. From afar, these look like sparkling blue gems strung together by silver threads.

The river formed by the confluence of the Kubi and Jiemayangzong, the Maquan (Horse Spring), derives its name from its colorful Tibetan appellation, Damqog Zangbo, meaning "river from the horse's ears"—a reference to the horsehead ridge at the glacier. The Maquan, its clear and shallow water teeming with fish, meanders eastward through verdant flats. It is named the Yarlung from Zhongba County. It travels in a comparatively straight line from its middle reaches on, accommodating itself to the structurally weaker area of the land along the suture line between the South Asian subcontinent (Gondwanaland) and the Eurasian continent (Laurasia).

Downstream from Saga, the river alternately widens and narrows as it cuts through several mountain ranges and passes through a series of gorges. The most famous among these include the Ganglai, Torxia, Yunda, Sangri-Gyaca, and Nangxian gorges. The precipitous walls confining the swift torrent are, for the most part, of solid granite. At a number of points, they come very close together. The narrowest part of the Ganglai Gorge, for example, is a little over 10 meters wide. Gigantic rocks protruding from the water along the 42-kilometer stretch of the Sangri-Gyaca Gorge give rise to rapids and cataracts that send spray flying 20 meters into the air. Both the proximity of the walls of the gorges and the exposed bedrock of the river at certain points offer excellent conditions for the construction of dams, where the violent flow of water could be put to use in generating a huge amount of hydroelectric power.

Each gorge is linked to the next by a broad valley. The two valleys stretching from Lhaze to Dag Chuka and from Quxu to Zetang are both 10 to 20 kilometers wide, but they have gradients of a mere 0.9 per mill and 0.27 per mill respectively. After plunging through the gorges, the river sprawls out lazily onto the river flats in the form of a typical braided stream.

The entire area, covering the middle reaches of the Yarlung and extending along the lower reaches of the tributaries that feed into the river from the north and south, lies below 4,000 meters in elevation, where temperatures are moderate and favorable for agriculture. For thousands of years, the main channel and its tributaries have watered the rich land on their banks, which, after generations of toil, has been turned by the Tibetans into excellent farmland. The earliest settlements were located here and gradually spread outward. Thus it is that the Yarlung Zangbo is considered the birthplace of Tibetan culture. The imposing Potala Palace by the Lhasa River, the golden Zhaxilhunbo Monastery within the city of Xigaze on the south bank of the Yarlung Zangbo channel, and the bastion outside the city of Gyangze by the Niyang River, which resisted British advances at the beginning of the century, are eloquent testimony to the superb civilization that blossomed forth on the river shores.

1. The riverbed of the lower Yarlung Zangbo is rasped away by the violent current. After piercing its way between two lofty snowy peaks in its eastern reaches, the river turns south around Mount Namjagbarwa, forming a big horseshoe bend. Namjagbarwa, 7,756 meters high, is on the right flank of the big bend and is the eastern terminus of the Himalayas.

Today, developments in modern technology can be observed in the industrial center of Nyingchi on the lower reaches of the Nyang River. New mining enterprises, factories, farms, and orchards can be seen all along the middle reaches of the Yarlung.

After gushing forth from the Nangxian Gorge, the Yarlung descends to an altitude of 3,000 meters, continuing its way eastward between wooded mountains. Downstream from Mainling, it is joined by the copious Niyang from the north. Now more vigorous than ever, it races along the foot of the eastern end of the Himalayan Range as it enters its lower stretch into an entirely different environment.

On reaching Pai in Mainling County, the river proceeds in a northeasterly direction, forming a canyon as it cuts its way between two formidable snowcapped peaks—Mount Jialabaili (7,151 meters), the summit of the Baishula Range, and to its south, Mount Namjagbarwa (7,756 meters), at the end of the Himalayan Range. The valley follows the bends formed by two series of fault lines crossed at right angles, producing a staircase effect. Before the sharp angles of the banks could be smoothened, the Plateau had already risen, making the river's violent waters cut deeper into the rock bed, so that the acute bends were left unchanged. The canyon then makes a U-turn and curls southwest around Mount Namjagbarwa, from which it twists into a spectacular zigzag. In this hazardous section of the huge vaulted valley, nature has created spectacular sights for the human eye, but, alas, has forgotten to leave a path, so that would-be explorers of the canyon's mysteries have, on many occasions, been compelled to turn back ungratified. However, our research team twice penetrated deep into the ravine to carry out multidisciplinary surveys under perilous conditions, and witnessed for the first time the marvels of this remote and fascinating region.

At the entrance of the canyon, the Yarlung is entrenched in murky, sunless depths between towering vertical walls of schist and gneiss. The upper part of the valley walls slopes gently before dropping abruptly into the ravine, so that the valley is ∨-shaped in cross-section. This is brought about by the strong downcutting force of the river. Because erosion in the adjoining lateral valleys did not keep up with the rapid cutting of the main valley, many tributaries have been left suspended high on the canyon walls, discharging their water in cascading streams a hundred meters or more into the Yarlung.

At higher altitudes, especially in the vicinity of Mount Jialabaili and Mount Namjagbarwa, lie vast glaciers reaching out in all directions. Because the speed at which the glaciers move far exceeds their rate of ablation, these huge masses of ice often thrust their way deep into forested areas or bamboo groves, and occasionally end within a mere hundred meters of the river's shores. As the glaciers move down the mountain valleys, they gouge out deep troughs in the bedrock. Frequently, segments of the perpendicular walls on either side collapse, setting off tremendous rockfalls into the valleys below, where the debris is carried by the glaciers down to the river's edge. Avalanches frequently occur, particularly downstream from the town of Jiala, where the riverbanks are so steep that blocks of snow and ice hurtle into the swift current below several times a day.

The northeasterly pressure of the South Asian continental plate, which is concentrated around the lower reaches of the Yarlung Zangbo, makes the earth's crust weak and unsettled in

2

this area, and thus particularly vulnerable to avalanches and rockfalls. In 1950, in the region of the canyon, there occurred an earthquake of 8.5 magnitude on the Richter scale which triggered extensive avalanches of rock, snow, and ice. The moving masses of detritus crushed forests and villages and clogged up rivers, drastically transforming the face of the land. Local inhabitants who survived this holocaust still shudder at the memory of it. One of the most striking consequences of the quake was the gouging of rock-laden valleys into mountain slopes. When an avalanche or some other mighty force stirs boulders and rocks into life, these roll down into the valleys and set off a chain reaction, whereby more and more rocks come tumbling down, shattering the silence of the mountains and merging to form terrifying rivers of moving stone. In 1973, near Baibung Village in Medog County, the precipice at the head of one of these valleys collapsed during a rainstorm, releasing a flow of rock and mud weighing over ten million tons. This huge mass moved down into the Yarlung Zangbo valley, where it blocked the river for a whole day, hindering its normal rapid flow.

The Yarlung Zangbo moves at an astounding rate of 10 meters per second between Mount Jialabaili and Mount Namjagbarwa. Here the torrents pound mercilessly against the rock, and waves cleave the air. The current in this deepest section of the valley gains momentum, dragging with it huge

2. A member of the research team crossing the billowing Yarlung by holding on to a cable suspended over the river.

3. Fording a stream of bone-chilling meltwater from a glacier in the vicinity of Mount Jialabaili in the eastern reaches of the Yarlung.

3

boulders which swiftly and rudely rasp down the riverbed, accounting for its vigorous and continuous downcutting. The fearful sounds of grinding rock, thundering avalanches of snow and ice, and roaring cascades all blend into a sonorous and awe-inspiring symphony that reverberates through the entire valley, shaking the very mountains.

The Yarlung leaves the Qinghai-Tibet Plateau as it descends the southern slope of the Himalayas. From Pai in Mainling County at the entrance of the canyon, to Xirang Village in Medog County at its exit, the river descends a total of 2,200 meters. This section of its course is 240 kilometers long. However, if a straight line were drawn between the two tips of the U-bend canyon, it would measure a mere 38 kilometers, so that, if a tunnel were to be dug through the Himalayas along this line, the river could be made to power a hydroelectric plant producing an astronomical 40,000 megawatts. It could be the mightiest power plant in the world. (The world's largest hydroelectric plant now in operation is at the Itaipu dam in Brazil, with an installed capacity of 12,600 megawatts.)

At a lower altitude farther downstream, near where the Jainzhug River joins the main channel from the east, the Yarlung stretches out into an elongated S and finally crosses the border into India, where it flows in a southwesterly direction as the Brahmaputra.

4

5

4. Far in the western part, or beginnings, of the Yarlung Zangbo system, the survey team sets up camp in Samsang at the confluence of the Jiemayangzong River from the north and the Kubi River from the south.

5. The Jiemayangzong glacier on the northern slopes of the Himalayas. From it springs the Jiemayangzong River, main source of the Yarlung Zangbo.

6

6. The Torxia Gorge below Dag Chuka, where the Yarlung has cut its way through the granite.

7. The most impressive city along the Yarlung ➤ Zangbo system, Lhasa is on a tributary to the north of the Yarlung. First built in the seventh century, the Potala Palace by the Lhasa River is a masterpiece of Tibetan architecture.

9

8. Surveying the Seng cascade in the Sangri-Gyaca Gorge. The cascade drops a total of 4.8 meters. In the narrowest part (39 meters) of the Sangri-Gyaca Gorge, the river's mean annual flow is 1,000 cubic meters per second.

9. The broad fertile flats along the middle stretch of the Yarlung Zangbo are Tibet's "granaries."

10

11

12

13

10. A steep glacier skirting Mount Jialabaili ends close to the river, in the big bend region. The glacier acts like a chute, from which ice and detritus deposited by avalanches slide 1,000 to 2,000 meters down into the Yarlung. Snow avalanches are a frequent phenomenon here, sometimes occurring several times a day.

11. The 7,151-meter Jialabaili, main peak of the Baishula Range, on the left side of the bend in the gorge.

12. A right-angle turn in the river's course, site of frequent landslides after the 1950 earthquake. A gigantic slumping of the river bank occurred here in 1972.

13. The roaring rapids of the big bend have tremendous hydropower potential.

15

14. Scaling a precipice by the Yarlung Zangbo.

15. At Baibung Village of Medog County, near the exit of the horseshoe bend, the Yarlung is about 600 meters above sea level. Here the climate is hot and the rainfall abundant.

17

18

16. Recording the flow in the horseshoe bend. The direction of the flow in the big bend is generally in conformity with the parallel arrangements of the texture of the schist and gneiss on the river's banks. The schistosity of the rocks in the region of the bend is, on the whole, large curved arcs that have Mount Namjagbarwa as their focal point. Frequently the river is here flanked by nearly vertical walls.

17. Fast-moving boulders and rocks from the slopes, or carried along by the tributaries of the Yarlung, gouge out huge chunks of the riverbed. The exposed texture of this quartz-schist rock, which at one stage had been part of the riverbed, shows long, deep grooves dug out of the mica-schist layers sandwiched between the harder quartz-schist layers; after the river receded, boulders that had been rubbed smooth and round were found in them.

18. The entrance to the horseshoe bend.

7
AZURE LAKES

Scattered about the lofty Qinghai-Tibet Plateau are numerous blue lakes and ponds. These bodies of water form the highest lake systems in the world and present some of China's most superb landscapes.

Each lake system has its own distinct history. The famous systems of East Africa arose with the fracturing of the earth's crust; most of the "thousand lakes" of Finland and those of Canada were formed by Quaternary glaciation. The formation of the Tibetan lakes, however, was not so simple. Their development correlates closely with the evolution of the Plateau's mountains and rivers; their diversity results from the rapid upward movement of the land and the enormous and complex geologic and morphological changes that took place during this crustal activity. Today, different stages of lake evolution can be observed in these countless lakes existing side by side.

The majority of the Plateau's lakes are of tectonic origin. The upheaval of the Plateau began more than 12 million years ago during the Pliocene epoch. High mountains rose on all sides, enclosing hollows which were later filled with water and became lakes. This was the first stage of lake formation on the Plateau. In the north, most of the lakes have an interior drainage system; in the south, an exterior drainage system. By the end of the early Pleistocene epoch, as tectonic movements in the crust reached a climax, the rate of elevation of the land varied in different areas. In certain areas where the upward movement was particularly pronounced a series of mountain ranges was built, and the intramontane depressions became natural water reservoirs. This was the second stage of lake formation. Examples of lakes formed as a direct consequence of tectonic activity are found in abundance on the North Tibet plateau, north of the Gangdise-Nyainqentanglha Range. Here, lakes may reach 4,600 meters in elevation and 2,000 square kilometers in area, as do the famous lakes Nam and Siling.

Some of the lakes on the Qinghai-Tibet Plateau were formed as a result of silting, or rock or lava blockages.

From the top of the mountain to the south of the Quxu Bridge spanning the Yarlung Zangbo, one has a panoramic view of Lake Yamzhog Yumco in the valley below. This odd-shaped lake, lying more than 800 meters above the river, appears

1. Climbers above a moraine lake on the north face of the Himalayas. Such a lake is formed when sediment left by retreating glaciers obstructs the flow of glacier meltwater.

as a dendritic network of waterways, with its main stem in the northwest branching out toward the southeast. Yamzhog Yumco was a tributary of the Yarlung until its course was blocked by mud and rock flows and sediment left by floods, creating a lake. Such a lake, whose intake is more or less balanced by evaporation, is called a barrier, or dammed, lake. Other factors, such as glaciation and tectonic movements, also contributed to the formation of Lake Yamzhog Yumco.

More dammed lakes have been formed in the southeastern part of the Plateau, where maritime glaciers are highly developed and rock falls and solifluctions of considerable size are common. (Solifluctions are the creeping of wet soil and rocks down a slope, resulting in the formation of terraces and mounds.) Lake Yiong on the lower reaches of the Yiong River and Lake Rawu on the upper reaches of the Youpu River are well-known examples. The abundant discharge of rivers in this part of the

Plateau often flows into the lakes and then flows out again over the blockage and seeping through it.

After the Holocene epoch, another retreat of mountain glaciers left behind terminal and lateral moraines, which obstructed the glacier valleys and held meltwater, forming moraine lakes. These, though small in area, are plentiful and are frequently seen at an altitude of over 5,500 meters.

On the northern part of the North Tibet plateau, volcanic activity has given rise to lava flows which have dammed up rivers to form lakes. Examples of these lava-dammed lakes, as they are termed, are Azhiqikkul and Ulukele, which were formed from a tributary of the Keriya River in Xinjiang, 4,600 meters above sea level in the Kunlun Range.

A feature worthy of mention is the extraordinary clarity and blueness of the lakes. The transparency of the water may reach as deep as 14 meters, far exceeding that of lakes in other parts of China. Various factors may account for this. First, temperatures on the Qinghai-Tibet Plateau are relatively low, so that vegetation is sparse and the humus content of the lakes consequently minimal. In addition, in the summer there are no torrential runoffs carrying silt and mud to cloud the water. Furthermore, the thin air of the Plateau at this altitude allows the sun's strong rays to penetrate deep into the lakes. As the light enters the water, the long-wave rays, such as red and yellow, are absorbed by the water particles, whereas the short-wave rays, such as green and blue, are dispersed and reflected back to the surface. The dazzling colors of these sapphirine lakes encircled by verdant shores and silver peaks lend a freshness and vitality to this magnificent region.

From a geochronological point of view, all lakes are short-lived. On the Qinghai-Tibet Plateau, those of the Pliocene epoch have been gradually reduced in volume, drained dry, or transformed into arid basins through evaporation. Most of the large tectonic lakes seen on the Plateau today originated during the second stage of lake formation toward the end of the early Pleistocene and reached their height of evolution in the interglacial period as the mid-Pleistocene drew to a close. Although these lakes are of diverse types and are constantly being added to by newly formed ones, the general tendency is for them to shrink. This phenomenon, which has been particularly marked within the last century, occurs more frequently in the northern part of the Plateau than in its southern part. Evidence of this shrinkage is borne by the lakes' ancient shorelines, which grow in number and in height as the altitude increases. For instance, whereas the uppermost ancient lake shoreline in the southern part of the Ngari Prefecture is a mere 30 to 40 meters above the present water level, that of the northern lakes is often 100 to 200 meters above the water surface. And there may be as many as twenty strand lines in one lake.

The diurnal temperature of the lakes, especially of those lying in inland basins, is more stable than the temperature on the surrounding land. During the day, air currents above the lakes move inland, but they reverse their direction at night. This atmospheric circulation carries vapor from the lakes over the land in the form of rain or dew, which nourishes the pastures and cropland on the banks. Temperatures in lake regions are higher than in other areas and therefore are conducive to agriculture and animal husbandry. Around Lake Tangra Yumco in North Tibet, highland barley grows well, despite the fact that the altitude here is beyond the normal limit for such crops.

Freshwater and semi-freshwater lakes teem with a scaleless or fine-scaled fish called the Schizothoracinae, descendants of the Tertiary carp. Its continual adaptation to the upward movement of the Plateau has resulted in its present morphology. Dissimilarities in the appearance of the various species of these scaleless carp reflect to a certain extent the different environmental changes that occurred during the process of upheaval in each of the regions they inhabit. The Schizothoracinae are a valuable aquatic resource of the Plateau.

Of even greater significance in terms of the Plateau's natural resources are the mineral salts found in its lakes. Throughout the existence of an inland lake, both surface and underground runoffs bring into it soluble salts which accumulate over the years. The water finally turns into brine, thus forming a salt lake—the declining stage of its development. Because the intake of these lakes cannot balance the amount lost through evaporation, the salt content becomes more concentrated and the physical and chemical conditions of the water change accordingly. Gradually, crystalline salts collect at the bottom of the lake in layers of varying thicknesses and composition, marking the different stages of the lake's salinization process.

Volcanic eruptions, magma intrusions, and hydrothermal activity, caused by movements within the Plateau's crust, have also played a part in bringing up to the surface rare substances in considerable amounts. Apart from the more common minerals such as rock salt, mirabilite, and gypsum, the lakes also contain large quantities of borax, a raw material indispensable to a number of industries. This mineral is rarely encountered in other parts of the world. Magnesium, potassium, and lithium, too, are found in high concentrations in these deposits, as are rubidium, cesium, strontium, uranium, and thorium.

The salt lakes of the Qinghai-Tibet Plateau are basins of tremendous mineral wealth. The extent of their resources is a fascinating subject that requires further exploration.

3

2

2. Deposits of white salts on a lake shore.

3. Borax on the shores of Salt Lake Cedo. Tibet has tremendous borax deposits.

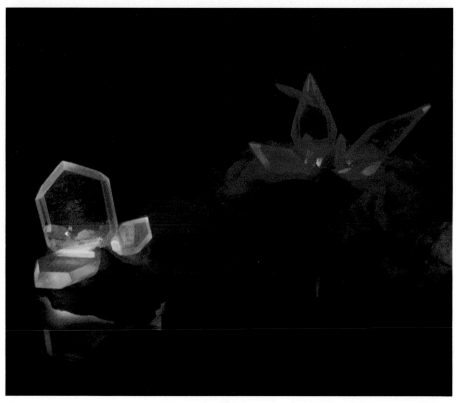

4

5

6

4. Hungtsaoite, first discovered in China, is quite commonly found in Tibetan lakes. It is one of the minerals containing borax.

5. Natural crystallized salt is used for making optical instruments.

6. Carnallite, a potassium-bearing mineral from an ancient salt lake.

7

8

9

7. Lakes Mapam Yumco (Saint's Lake) and Langa (Devil's Lake) are in Ngari Prefecture between the Himalayas and the Gangdise Range. At one time these formed one lake which drained into the Langqen River. As the water receded, it was cut into two interior draining lakes connected only by a thin strip of water. Lake Mapam Yumco is over 80 meters deep; it is a Buddhist shrine where, in summer, pilgrims from abroad come to worship.

8. Most of Lake Bangong in Ngari Prefecture on China's western border lies within Chinese territory. This long and narrow lake is fed mainly by rivers from the east. The water in its western end is salty and undrinkable as a result of evaporation and the lake's narrow width. Lake Bangong is a tectonic lake in an east-west fault whose faces are still clearly discernible.

9. Most lakes in Tibet are shrinking and have left rings of ancient strand lines.

10

10. Salt Lake Margai on the North Tibet plateau is a shallow salt lake with a solid bed of white mineral salts. To transport our matériel to the other side of the lake, we loaded it into a rubber boat and dragged the boat across without much trouble.

11. Lake Yamzhog Yumco, south of the Yarlung Zangbo, is the largest freshwater lake in southern Tibet. The lake, which is 624 square kilometers in area with a storage capacity of 15 billion cubic meters of water, flowed into the Yarlung until it was dammed by a rockfall. Lying 4,440 meters above sea level and 800 meters higher than the nearby Yarlung, it has a considerable hydropower potential.

13

12. Nam Co, Tibetan for "celestial lake," is a brackish body of water measuring 1,920 square kilometers in area. It lies 4,718 meters above sea level on the northern slopes of the Nyainqentanglha Range.

13. Lake Yiong, 2,150 meters above sea level, was dammed by a rockfall in the early 1900s. Situated in the eastern part of the Plateau, where the climate is mild and the rainfall abundant, it has thick forests covering its banks.

8 ALPINE PLANTS

The term "alpine plants" is a general name for all vegetation that grows above the timberline. On the Qinghai-Tibet Plateau, this line is at 4,500 meters above sea level. At this altitude, trees give way to countless species of shrubs and herbaceous plants. In the blossoming season, their brilliantly colored flowers flutter in the wind just below icy mountain peaks, on sheer cliffs, and in rocky wastes. Some even push up from under the snow. The precise upper limit at which alpine plants can survive is not yet known, but our research team saw flocks of goats grazing at 5,800 meters, and even at 6,000 meters we found bush cinquefoil.

In the course of evolution, the alpine plants have developed many varieties and have acquired adaptive characteristics that enable them to withstand the harsh environment.

Lichens, a group of lower plants that attach themselves to outcroppings of rock, are the pioneers at high altitudes. By secreting lichen acid they dissolve and fragment the rocks into the most primitive form of soil, extracting nutrients for themselves and at the same time creating the basic conditions for the existence of other plants. Mosses grow on the debris of the dead lichens. They perform photosynthesis more efficiently than the lichens and multiply quickly, producing a further accumulation of fine soil and organic matter. This lays the foundation for the growth of higher plants.

Many of the alpine plants branch close to the ground in the shape of compact cushions. A cushion-like shrub is generally no more than 60 to 70 centimeters tall, but its crown may have a diameter of 7 to 8 meters. This shape protects the underlying soil from excessive evaporation and enables the plant to absorb maximum heat during the hours of direct sunlight and to retain heat at night. Thus the plants have a relatively stable moisture content and temperature. For example, we found that when the outside temperature dropped below freezing, the temperature inside the plants remained above the freezing point.

Most of these cushion-shaped species are herbaceous plants, such as rock jasmine and sandwort, which grow in clusters on otherwise barren plateaus. But the cushion plants also include shrubs, such as pea shrub, honeysuckle, and goosefoot, and even dwarfed trees, such as willow and juniper. Willows, which

1. The beneficial properties of medicinal plants have been known to the people of Tibet since ancient times. This picture, painted on cloth, dates from the seventeenth century, but it is said to have been copied from a much older original that was painted on bark. The renderings are so accurate that they were used to illustrate the *Encyclopaedia of Medicine,* a classic of Tibetan medicine and pharmacology.

grow to a height of dozens of meters in more hospitable regions, may be only a third of a meter tall at these altitudes. A two-hundred-year-old juniper may sprawl on the ground, achieving a height of less than a meter.

Certain plants, such as edelweiss, *Saussurea,* and *Nepeta,* are covered with a soft, fine, hairy growth, the fibers of which mat together to form innumerable tiny chambers. There is almost no interchange between the air inside and outside these chambers. Thus, they form an insulating shell that protects the plant against loss of water through rapid evaporation and acts as a buffer against the strong solar radiation.

Other alpine plants have leaves that are specifically adapted to the dry, cold climate. The leaves of Tibetan rhubarb, Tibetan draba, *Lamiophlomia rotata,* Tibetan figwort, and *Przewalskia tangutica,* which is found nowhere else in the world, grow in clusters at the base of their stems, holding close to the ground in the shape of open lotus blossoms. This structure enables the plants to resist high winds, slow down evaporation, and obtain heat from the earth's surface.

Others, like stonecrop, have thick fleshy leaves that retain water and protect them from dehydration and freezing. Stonecrop has another curious way of adapting to the environment: every year its stem dries up but does not fall. A new stem simply grows up in the middle of the old one, so that in time the old stems come to form a thick protective coating, guarding the plant against the wind and cold. The sagebrush curls up its leaves into tiny needle-like tubes, a shape that reduces the plant's respiration and the loss of water through evaporation.

All the alpine plants have well-developed roots for absorbing water and nutrients. For example, the pagoda-shaped rhubarb plant, which grows on rock-strewn mountain slopes, has roots over a meter long, longer even than its flowering stem. The stiffleaf sedge, which dominates some parts of the North Tibet plateau, attains a height of only 10 to 30 centimeters, but its roots may extend for 150 centimeters.

In the struggle to survive, some alpine plants take advantage of the brief growing season and complete their life cycle in the shortest possible time. Plants like *Pegoeophyton scapiflorum*

2. Professor Wu Zhengyi (*center*), a noted botanist, has made two research trips to Tibet. He is pictured collecting samples with his colleagues.

sprout, flower, bear fruit, and wither—all in the space of one month or even less.

Unlike most of the Qinghai-Tibet Plateau, the southern and southeastern portions are favored with sufficient rainfall and a relatively mild climate. There the alpine plants grow in astonishing variety. We found twenty of China's twenty-four species of *Saussurea,* and no less than sixty to seventy species of alpine rhododendron, along with many other plants, including primrose, gentian, saxifrage, and rock jasmine. On the North Tibet plateau, particularly its northwestern part, where there is an annual rainfall of only 20 millimeters, there is naturally less vegetation. Yet even there we found needlegrass and sagebrush grasslands, goosefoot, false tamarisk, colorful milk vetch, crimson *Weigela,* and many others.

The alpine plants not only bring beauty to the Plateau, they also are a source of wealth for its inhabitants. Among them are valuable medicinal herbs, such as fritillary, point vetch, Asia bell, Tibetan figwort, and *Bergenia,* which have been known and used in traditional Tibetan medicine for hundreds of years. Even more precious than these are the humble grasses; providing varied types of pasture in different areas at different seasons, they support the herds and flocks that are indispensable to the people of the Plateau.

4

5

3

3. This vast region below the snow line and above the tree line is the realm of the alpine plants. During blossomtime, they burst forth in brilliant color against a background of glistening snow.

4. Alpine primrose.

5. The Himalayan cassiope grows in bushy grassland 4,200 meters above sea level. One of the shortest shrubs, it has a stem less than 20 centimeters long.

6

9

7

10

11

8

6. Tibetan rock jasmine.

7. Setose rhododendron. Of the 600 to 700 species of rhododendron in the world, 400 to 500 can be found in the mountains of southeastern China. There are over 270 species in Tibet alone, not including the tree rhododendrons that grow in the forests. Early in spring, at altitudes above 4,500 meters, they cover the mountains with their gorgeous flowers of red, purple, yellow, and white. The small, thick leaves of the alpine rhododendrons contain a volatile aromatic substance that has recently been found to be effective in the treatment of bronchitis and asthma.

8. Cinquefoil growing in the shape of a cushion, on the north slope of the Himalayas, 5,100 meters above sea level.

9. On mountain slopes that receive adequate rainfall, many species of brightly colored flowers adorn the meadows.

10. *Chesneya nubigena* is widely distributed in the southern part of Tibet, at elevations of about 4,500 meters.

11. Common *Bergenia*, which grows on mountain slopes 4,000 meters above sea level, helps reduce inflammations.

12

13

14

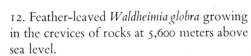

15

12. Feather-leaved *Waldheimia globra* growing in the crevices of rocks at 5,600 meters above sea level.

13. Stonecrop growing near the source of the Yarlung Zangbo.

14. *Pedicularis globifera*. Its root is a tonic.

15. Chinese poppy. Plants of the genus *Meconopsis* are flowering herbs commonly used in Tibetan medicine. They have large, showy flowers of red, yellow, purple, and blue. Of the forty species in the world, about twenty can be found in Tibet, some growing on grassland at the edge of forests, others in rock crevices on high mountains or on rock-strewn slopes.

16

17

18

19

20

21

16. In the valley 4,800 meters above sea level at the foot of Mount Kangrinboqe, the principal peak of the Gangdise Mountains, stonecrop, saxifrage, *Crementhodium,* and many other plants bloom in July before the snow melts.

17. A pagoda-shaped rhubarb. This plant grows to a height of about one meter on rocky mountainsides. Its yellow calyxes resemble flower petals.

18. Gentian is used to reduce fever and inflammations.

19. Tibetan delphinium, effective against dysentery and diarrhea.

20. The bulb of fritillary, which grows in abundance in the southeastern part of Tibet, is used to reduce fever and as a cough medicine.

21. *Saussurea* dominates uninhabited areas of North Tibet at 5,000 meters above sea level.

22

23

24

22. *Pedicularis* blooming in the snow.

23. Yellow Chinese poppies blossoming on a flint-covered slope at 4,500 meters. This herb is used as a cough remedy.

24. Snow lotus, one of the many species of the genus *Saussurea,* thrives near the snow line at 5,000 meters above sea level. It blossoms before the ice and snow are completely melted.

25

26

27

28

29

30

31

25. Milk vetch, which grows on the sandy slopes of the North Tibet plateau 4,700 to 5,200 meters above sea level, has small, hairy leaves but bears giant seeds—a special feature of certain plants on the Qinghai-Tibet Plateau.

26. *Oreosolen wattii* is used to reduce fever.

27. *Thylacospermum caespitosum.*

28. *Thylacospermum caespitosum* growing in clusters at 5,500 meters, on the Nganglong Mountains of Ngari Prefecture.

29. Only goosefoot and compact false tamarisk thrive in the alkaline valley, 4,800 meters above sea level, between the Karakorum and the Kunlun mountains in the north Ngari Prefecture.

30. False tamarisk in the Zada valley of Ngari.

31. Cushion-shaped sandwort.

9
THE
GRASSLANDS
OF TIBET

Grassland makes up 70 percent of the total land area of Tibet. Because the climate and geographic features vary greatly from one part of the region to another, the grassland is of different sorts, depending upon its locality. It can be divided into four principal types.

1. Mountain grassland: In the upper section of the Yarlung Zangbo valley, between the Himalayas and the Gangdise Mountains, the climate is moderate compared with that of the North Tibet plateau. Here grow the grass species of the temperate zone. On the level ground by the river, *Pennisetum* and *Orinus thorolii* predominate, while on the valley slopes various species of drought-resistant grass thrive. Among the most common of these are awned needlegrass, purple-flowered needlegrass, and the three-awn variety.

2. Alpine meadows: These are found on the high mountains in the central and eastern part of Tibet, where the winds are strong and there is no absolutely frost-free period. Every year, as soon as the brief warm season begins, stubby grass of the sedge family and different species of the sagebrush spring up from the moist earth. Their growth is sparse and stunted, and they have a strong root system which loosens the earth. Accounting for 39 percent of the total grassland area of Tibet, alpine meadows are Tibet's best grazing grounds.

3. Plateau and wide valley grassland: This is located mainly in the North Tibet plateau at about 4,500 meters above sea level, where the climate is cold and dry. Immense grassland areas here are covered with purple-flowered needlegrass, which can withstand these climatic conditions. However, the grass coverage is only 30 percent, and the fresh-grass yield totals 300 kilograms per hectare. When the needlegrass flowers in August, its feathery spikes turn the grassland into a stretch of glittering white.

4. Marshy meadows: These are scattered across the vast grassland where there are small pools and dank low-lying ground. They are small, and lie in warmer temperatures than the surrounding higher land. The grass here sprouts earlier than elsewhere, and grows so bountifully that the per-hectare yield may be as much as two to three and a half tons. The pre-dominating grass is Tibetan sagebrush, which puts forth its

1. Taking grass samples and measuring the yield.

stalks from the base of the plant or from the axils of its lower leaves above the ground in tufts. These marshy grazing grounds supply Tibetan herdsmen with fresh fodder just when it is needed most—at the close of the long winter, when the last year's grass has been consumed.

On most parts of the Qinghai-Tibet Plateau, the grass is short and sparse in comparison with, for example, the deep, luxuriant plants that cover the Hulun Buir Grassland in Inner Mongolia. However, the strong solar radiation on the Plateau speeds up the process of photosynthesis, so that the grasses there are particularly high in nutritional value, containing as much as 16.8 percent coarse protein. Furthermore, their low yield is counterbalanced by the variety of the different types

of grassland that lie within close proximity of each other.
The fact that grass is available at different times is a special
advantage for Tibetan herdsmen, for it enables them to tide
their animals over the seasonal shortage in fodder. The herdsmen
have an old saying that reflects the use they make of this
wide availability of fodder: "Graze your herds on the hilltops
in summer and down the valleys in winter. When autumn
comes, drive them up the mountains to gain more weight."

The Qinghai-Tibet Plateau is one of China's five major stock-
raising areas. The climate of the different parts of the Plateau is
so varied that almost every kind of domesticated animal, with
the exception of the camel, is raised in one region or another.
The most important economically are yaks, sheep, and cattle.

The yak is the most important animal of the Plateau.
Because they have strong legs and tough hooves, yaks can carry
heavy loads for long distances on the rocky mountains; thus
they are fondly referred to as "ships of the Plateau." Yaks are
also used to pull plows in the farming areas. Cow yaks do not
milk as well as ordinary cows, but their tasty yellowish milk has
a fat content of 6 to 8 percent. Tents made from yak-hair felt
are strong enough to withstand wind and rain. The heavy
woolen locally machine-made cloth from the fine hair of yaks
sells well on the domestic market. Highly resistant to cold
climate, yaks are seen grazing on the North Tibet plateau when
the temperature drops to −30° C. However, they cannot stand
the summer heat. When the temperature rises to 15° to 20° C,
they begin to gasp for breath, and are unable to eat any grass.

Of all the livestock on the Plateau, sheep are the most
plentiful. The best-known variety is the Tibetan sheep,
raised throughout the Yarlung Zangbo valley. The fine
elastic wool of this sheep is handwoven into *pulu*—a warm,
heavy cloth that is much prized all over the Plateau.

Animals on the Plateau are thoroughly acclimatized to the
alpine conditions of severe cold and rarefied air, because they
have bigger lungs, underdeveloped sweat glands, and thick fur.
Moreover, their blood contains more red cells than animals
of low altitudes. Red blood cells are oxygen carriers. When the
density of oxygen is low, the number of red cells multiplies to
enable the normal amount of oxygen to be carried to the tissues.

The table below shows that the number of red cells in the blood of sheep increases with the altitude at which they graze:

Altitude (meters)	Number of Red Blood Cells (per cubic millimeter)
Below 1,000	9 million
3,600 (in Tibet)	10.93 million
4,200	12.37 million

Although the strains of animals on the Plateau are good in general, to raise their productivity and the quality of animal products fine breeds from other parts of China have been introduced.

While the wool from Tibetan sheep is good enough for coarse clothing and rugs, it cannot be used for spinning. So, in 1962, fine-wool and semifine-wool sheep were introduced for crossbreeding. The experiment has been a success: wool from the new generation of sheep matches that of the Inner Mongolian sheep in quality and surpasses that of the local sheep in quantity. At about the same time, fine-breed cows from the Hulun Buir Grassland in Inner Mongolia were introduced to the Plateau to improve the local breed. They have become gradually acclimatized to the harsh elements and high altitudes. Their crossbred offspring are an average of 10 centimeters taller than the local cattle, and they give from three to four times as much milk.

2. At 4,200 meters above sea level, meadows of sagebrush interspersed with chrysanthemums and other flowering plants are seen on the mountain slopes. Alpine meadows have a bountiful yield and are the best grazing grounds of Tibet in the summer and autumn.

3

4

3. Covered with thick, long hair, yaks can withstand persistent roughage, alpine cold, and rarefied air. Male yaks are particularly strong, highly irascible, and difficult to manage.

4. Stud bulls of the Binzhou breed, grazing by the Nyang River near Nyingchi in southeast Tibet. Binzhou cattle of the Hulun Buir Grassland in northeastern China are bulky and provide good beef and milk. They have acclimatized themselves well to the alpine conditions of the Qinghai-Tibet Plateau since their introduction to the region.

5. A herd of yaks grazing on the wide valley grassland of the North Tibet plateau.

6. Tibetan horses are stocky, and can travel long distances over rocky mountains.

5

6

7

7. The Ngari horse of west Tibet is an improved breed of the Tibetan horse.

8. Tibetan sheep are an offshoot of the sheep ➤ of northwest China. They have a long, elastic wool which is good material for carpet-weaving.

10 FORESTS— THE PLATEAU'S GREEN TREASURY

If one traverses the high mountains of the southern Hengduan Range or penetrates the valleys of the lower Yarlung Zangbo, one will find oneself immersed in a sea of virgin forests fringing China's southwest border. This is the Tibet Forest Zone, a vast green treasure-trove whose value has not yet been fully revealed.

After the Oligocene epoch, the South Asian plate floated north from the southern hemisphere and eventually coalesced with the Eurasian plate. The force generated by the collision of the two plates pushed the land upward to form the vast Qinghai-Tibet Plateau. During the subsequent Quaternary period, the alternating glacial and interglacial periods that occurred in the northern hemisphere complicated the migration, mixture, and differentiation of the forest plants of the elevated Plateau, resulting in the rich and variegated tree species there. The different climatic conditions of the Tibet Forest Zone have made it possible for a wide variety of vegetation to flourish, including more than fifty forest formations and a still greater number of forest types. It is indeed rare for such diverse vegetation to be concentrated in one region.

Under the influence of their monsoon climate, the deep mountain valleys and secluded ravines became the sanctuary of a number of ancient species of forest trees. According to the preliminary investigations of our research team, there are at present over 1,300 species of tall trees and shrubs in the Tibet Forest Zone. These can be classified under more than 100 families and 300 genera. Among these, there are conifers of high economic value, which alone belong to 8 families, 16 genera, and over 40 species. In addition to those species of conifer that can be found in other provinces, such as the Yunnan pine, alpine pine, armand pine, west Sichuan spruce, and yellow-cone Likiang spruce, there are 15 species which can be found only in Tibet. The most common of these are the Himalayan pine, long-leaf pine, long-leaf spruce, Himalayan fir, Himalayan larch, and Himalayan cypress.

The conifers are exceptionally tall and erect. Their straight-grained, water-resistant wood with its high tensile strength makes excellent timber for furniture and building purposes. This type of forest tree is particularly sturdy and, at

1. Members of the research team discussing their work in the forest.

the same time, is endowed with a unique beauty. The spike fir, for instance, locally known as "*xierangxing*," survived the violent climatic changes of the Quaternary period. Its long, broad leaves have on their lower surface two distinct rows of breathing pores, while its seeds have a scarlet coating. This precious plant, as the living fossil of its ancient species, is rarely encountered elsewhere and is very much treasured as a decorative and afforested tree species.

On slopes which have a temperate or subtropical climate, broadleaf trees predominate. The rhododendron, rose, and legume families are the dominant ones of this group, followed by the honeysuckle, willow, camphor, and cupule families. Of these, the camphor tree, *Phoebe nanmu,* magnolia, Chinese toon, oak, and mountain ash all furnish excellent wood. Some of them are noted for their beautiful coloration; others are famous for their fine-textured hardwood; still others, for their aroma. All provide first-rate material for furniture and building.

The tropical evergreen broadleaf forests also include many valuable species of hardwood broadleaf trees which supply high-quality material for making durable furniture and tools.

The timber reserve of the Tibet Forest Zone averages 220 cubic meters per hectare, the highest in the whole country.

As one passes through the zone, one often comes upon colossal trees whose tips seem to touch the very clouds. Some spruce and fir trees reach above 70 meters, equaling the height of a twenty-storied building. It would take six persons, standing on the ground with arms outstretched, to encircle the trunk of one of these trees. Such a tree can yield as much as 40 cubic meters of timber. It would require ten trucks, each with a ten-ton capacity, to transport such a huge quantity.

Most of the trees grow at a remarkably rapid rate and continue to do so over a fairly long duration. Those that grow most rapidly are the Himalayan pine, long-leaf pine, Yunnan pine, and armand pine. In a relatively favorable environment, trees between 20 and 40 years old can increase by more than 1 centimeter in diameter and 1 meter in height each year. For example, the Yunnan pine in the Zayu area, in southeast Tibet, takes a mere 130 years to attain an average breast-height diameter of 72.3 centimeters, a height of about

2. The Himalayan cypress is a tree species peculiar to the valleys of the middle reaches of the Yarlung. Of moderate height, some of these trees have trunks whose breast-height diameter is 4 meters.

50 meters, and a per-hectare timber reserve of 1,000 cubic meters. By contrast, the red pine, the chief timber-producing tree in the Lesser Hinggan Mountains in northeast China, requires 220 years to reach a breast-height diameter of 46 centimeters, a height of 29 meters, and a per-hectare timber reserve of 800 cubic meters. The spruce of the Bomi area, in eastern Tibet, can, under the genial climatic conditions of the valleys, also yield high timber reserve—over 2,000 cubic meters per hectare.

The rapid growth and fine wood-yield of trees in the Tibet Forest Zone are accounted for by the propitious climatic conditions of southeastern Tibet. The major part of the zone is located on the south side of the Plateau's mountains, which directly faces the northerly monsoons traveling from the Indian Ocean. The winds bring with them an abundant amount of water at a time when the forest plants are in their growing season. After the monsoons, when the dry season sets in, the valleys and mountains are enveloped in clouds and mists, which, to a certain extent, compensate for the shortage of moisture. Because the lofty Plateau is blessed with intense solar radiation, a low latitude, and an immense accumulation of heat, the Tibet Forest Zone has abnormally high temperatures for winter, reducing the possibility of damage by extreme cold, and affording exceptionally favorable conditions for tree growth and better quality of timber. Since temperatures vary little throughout the year, plants can grow over a long period of time. In summer, heat waves, which could be detrimental to tree growth, are scarce. Furthermore, the great difference in temperature between day and night accelerates the absorption of nourishment.

Because the virgin forests of Tibet have so far been kept intact, they are rarely afflicted with plant diseases or infested with insect pests. Trees which grow in areas below the alpine belt have a particularly low rate of decay, a phenomenon that is without parallel in other forest zones of the country.

4

5

3. Glossy *Ganoderma*, a precious medicinal fungus. It thrives under alpine oaks that predominate on slopes of 3,000 meters above sea level around the horseshoe bend of the Yarlung, where rain is plentiful and the climate genial.

4. Glossy *Ganoderma*—a close-up.

5. "Monkey's head," a kind of mushroom which grows on trees, is a rare delicacy. Subsidiary products like this are plentiful in Tibet's forests.

6

6. A coniferous forest of firs and hemlocks on the south face of Mount Namjagbarwa, 2,400 to 3,700 meters above sea level. Sturdy and handsome, the firs are a major feature of the subalpine coniferous forest.

7. Extensive tropical forests grow on slopes of less than 1,000 meters in elevation around Medog, by the lower Yarlung. They form the northernmost limit of tropical forests in Eurasia.

8

9

8. The virgin forest of the Himalayas. The southeast part of Tibet is occupied by one of China's major virgin forests. Here the vegetation forms are diversified; the various species of trees grow very fast; and the per-hectare timber reserve is very large. The entire area is of great importance in both economic and environmental terms.

9. The long-leaf spruce is a tree species peculiar to the Himalayas. Growing below 2,800 meters of elevation in Gyirong County, it appears in mixed forests with other broadleaf and needle-leaf trees.

10. The spruce forest in the valleys of Bomi. The tallest tree may reach a height of over 70 meters, with a trunk diameter of over 2 meters. Its per-hectare timber reserve exceeds 2,000 cubic meters.

11

12

11. Cypresses are sparse and stunted in areas where forests give way to meadows or alpine scrubs.

12. Growing fast and furnishing fine wood, the Himalayan pine is an important tree species on the south face of the Himalayas within the boundary of China.

13. In central and eastern Tibet, on mountain slopes between 2,500 and 3,500 meters above sea level, there are alpine forests of orderly shape. The alpine pine, which grows very fast, is one of the chief sources of timber.

11
MOUNT NAMJAGBARWA— NATURE'S FLORAL SHOWCASE

As one treks southward on the Qinghai-Tibet Plateau, crossing the Duoxiongla Pass of Mount Namjagbarwa at the eastern end of the Himalayas and descending to the deep valleys of the Yarlung Zangbo, one undergoes the unique experience of witnessing the four distinct seasons of the year in the short space of two to three days.

Once the pass is reached, the traveler is chilled, even if it is spring or summer, by the freezing winds that blow across the surrounding snowcapped summits. As he descends the steep mountain slope, however, the increasingly hotter weather will cause him to doff successive layers of outer clothing. When he finally reaches the iron-chain bridge spanning the Yarlung at Medog, he will find himself bathed in sweat as the sun blazes down mercilessly upon him. With the change in climatic conditions, he will have noticed an increasingly richer variety of plant species. Medog (Tibetan for "flower") County, on the banks of the Yarlung, offers, as its name indicates, a particularly lush display of green vegetation and colorful blossoms.

Hemmed in on three sides by the looping river and rising to a colossal height of 7,756 meters, Mount Namjagbarwa presents a complete vertical zonation of vegetation forms that appear in the humid areas of the northern hemisphere, ranging from plants of the alpine snowbound belt to those of the low-mountain tropical belt.

In the tranquillity of the summit, around the lower fringe of this apparently lifeless snowbound world, grows and multiplies the variegated snow-alga. Close to the snow line at an altitude of 5,000 meters, the mean annual temperature is about 0° C. When the snow thaws, a number of seed plants begin to sprout on the craggy slopes. They include the woolly snow lotus and integrifolious poppy, the succulent-leaved red stonecrop and the cushion-like white sandwort. Besides these, the alpine meadows are covered with tiny-leaved, short-stemmed plants and shrubs such as the rhododendron, willow, primrose, saxifrage, and gentian. Altogether they form a huge resplendent wreath around the base of the mountain's snow crown.

Between 2,300 and 3,700 meters above sea level, the climate is temperate and humid, with the mean annual temperature ranging from 3° to 11° C. Here, the tall and dense needle-leaf and mixed needle- and broadleaf forests encircle the waist of Mount Namjagbarwa like a wide emerald girdle. The upper half of the girdle consists chiefly of firs. Their needle-like leaves spread out in all directions to intercept the sunshine before it reaches the ground. As a result, the soil is cold and dank and covered with moss which spreads like a soft, thick carpet over the forest floor. The firs are interspersed with honeysuckles, maples, European bird cherries, and glossy-leaf Chinese canes, as well as a profusion of rosebushes bearing countless buds. Ditches and roads are lined with raspberry bushes, whose piquantly sour berries are irresistible to every passerby. In the lower half of the girdle, where precipitation is greater, sturdy hemlocks stretch out their drooping branchlets festooned with tassel-like epiphytes such as *Usnea*. In summer the forests, immersed in thick clouds and fog, become even darker and more humid. Tree trunks are covered with moss and ferns; edible mushrooms spring up among fallen twigs and thick piles of leaves, along with clusters of *Plagiogyria* and clearweed with pellucid and water-saturated stems and leaves. But perhaps most outstanding are the red-bark rhododendrons. These plants grow into 12-meter-tall trees with thick, crooked branches and twigs.

The climate is even warmer and more humid in the region between 1,800 and 2,300 meters above sea level, where the mean annual temperature stands at 12° to 16° C. The precipitation is also greater than that of the region immediately above. Here, in the evergreen broadleaf forests, the lamellape evergreen oak of the cupule family predominates, with an admixture of tall camphor and *Phoebe nanmu* trees. In contrast to the pinnacle of the conifers, each treetop is a rounded canopy. The tree trunks are coated with moss dotted here and there with leaf fern, while *Agapetes mannii* and wild black pepper cling to their branches. The shrubby undergrowth here consists mainly of bamboos, including a species that has a ring of thorns growing around its nodes.

Below 1,800 meters, the atmosphere is much clearer. Preponderant among the forest trees here are the evergreen chinquapins, which are over 30 meters tall. These have centipede tongavine gripping their trunks and clusters of huge-leaved wild bajiao bananas growing in the shade of their foliage. The betel nut palm of the palm family, representative of the southern subtropical region, appears at a height of 1,600 meters above sea level. Farther down, at an altitude of 1,300 meters, the *Cyathea*, a genus of tree fern, appears. This plant with a woody stem is the descendant of an ancient species that flourished 70 million years ago in the warm and humid climate of the Mesozoic era. Although it died out in other parts of Tibet during the repeated glacial periods of the Quaternary period, it has survived in southeast Tibet because of the area's peculiar monsoon climate and geomorphological conditions.

Below an altitude of 1,100 meters, the valleys present spectacular tropical landscapes. The mountain slopes are cut into tidy, green, terraced fields. The wooden huts of the Monbas, who inhabit this area, are tucked away among tall

Vertical Zonation of Vegetation of Mount Namjagbarwa, Eastern Himalayas

The southeastern part of Tibet, with its towering mountains and deep valleys, shows a vast range of altitudes. The distance between Mount Namjagbarwa and Baibung Village in the Yarlung Zangbo valley is a mere 45 kilometers, yet the difference in elevation is more than 7,000 meters. All the vegetation forms occurring in the humid areas of the northern hemisphere, from those of the cool temperate zone to those of the tropics, appear in orderly succession on the mountain slopes as they decrease in altitude.

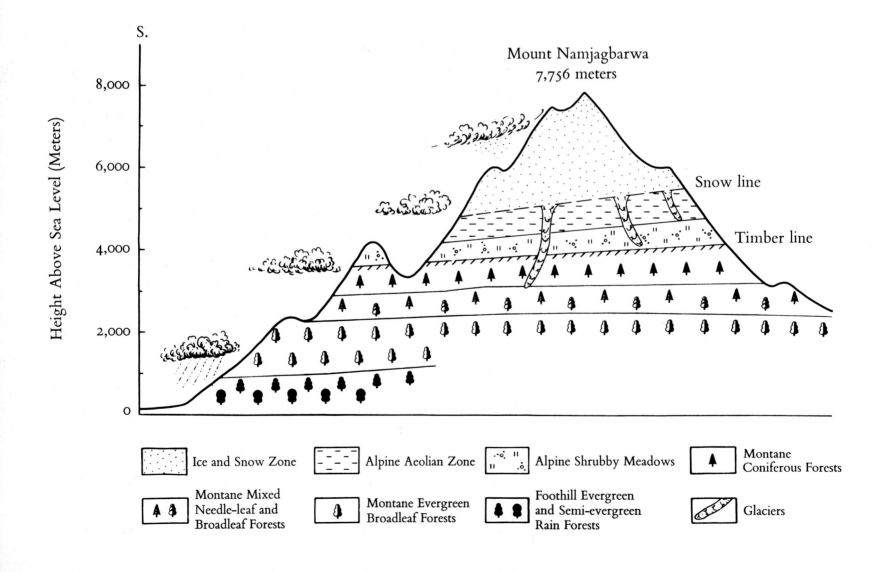

S.

Mount Namjagbarwa
7,756 meters

Height Above Sea Level (Meters)

8,000

6,000

Snow line

Timber line

4,000

2,000

0

Ice and Snow Zone   Alpine Aeolian Zone   Alpine Shrubby Meadows   Montane Coniferous Forests

Montane Mixed Needle-leaf and Broadleaf Forests   Montane Evergreen Broadleaf Forests   Foothill Evergreen and Semi-evergreen Rain Forests   Glaciers

banana trees and wild orange, tangerine, and lemon groves. Here, summer is exceptionally long. Winter is nonexistent, with the mean annual temperature standing at 16° to 18° C. The lowest temperature is well above zero; thus there is no word for "ice" in the vocabulary of the Monbas. The moisture-laden air currents coming from the Bay of Bengal in the south move up to the valleys, resulting in an annual precipitation here of more than 2,000 millimeters.

In the tropical virgin forests that spread far and wide over this area, there grow a great variety of plants, with no one species predominating. Trees, shrubs, epiphytes, and creepers are intricately intertwined, presenting a wondrous sight of lush verdure. The highest tier of vegetation in these forests consists of the canopies of the evergreen broadleaf trees such as the tropical-almond *Terminalia*, southwest crape myrtle, *Homalium*, and the many kinds of banyans, whose striking features are their straight trunks; smooth, light-colored bark; and the 2- to 3-meter high, plank-like buttresses which have developed around their trunks. The southwest crape myrtle is particularly outstanding in appearance. With a height of 40 meters, it does not branch till two-thirds of the way up. Its smooth, light-green trunk presents a challenge even to the most agile of monkeys; hence its nickname "*dergongxing*," which, in the dialect of the Monbas, means "too difficult for the monkeys to climb."

Trees of secondary height include the twinflower *Abelia*, heliotrope *Ehretia*, and Chinese *Altingia*. Some of these have thread-like air roots hanging from their boughs. Others bear fruits that grow directly out of their branches and twigs—a phenomenon which the local people describe as "flowering on the old stems." The *Gynocardia odorata* of the chaulmoogra family, for instance, which is called "*apidu*" in the dialect of the Monbas, is laden with yellow fruits the size of apples.

All these features—the plank-like buttresses, the air roots, and the "flowering on the old stems"—are characteristic of tropical rain-forest trees.

There is an even greater variety of lianas in the forests, including the palm, grape, legume, and gourd families. Their long vines entwine themselves around the trunks of the tall trees standing nearby. Ferns, mosses, and orchids also cling to the trunks of the trees or sometimes nestle in their crotches, making their straight trunks look swollen and ungainly.

These dense tropical forests contain a multitude of plants that can serve specific purposes. Among the most precious medicinal herbs are cardamom, used for treating gastric troubles; *Entada*, for nephritis; *Choerospondias axillaris* and betel pepper, for cardiac diseases; *Clerodendron serralum spreng,* a species of glory bower, used to prevent malaria; the gambier plant, for rheumatism; and *Dendrobium nobile,* a species of orchid, for indigestion.

Plants of commercial value are also found in abundance here. The kernel of the *Hodgsonia macrocarpa,* which tastes of peanuts and is used to stop bleeding and help swellings subside, contains 77 percent oil, is also of use in industry. The fibers of the *Sterculia nobilis* can be used as diversely as hemp. Vines and bamboos serve as good material in weaving handicraft and household articles such as baskets and chairs. In the vicinity of Medog, there is a bridge over the Yarlung Zangbo made of interlaced white vines of the palm family, each 20 to 30 meters long. The wild oranges, citrons, and eared strangler figs are all edible fruit. The intense heat and rich moisture here are extremely conducive to the growth of tropical plants of high economic value. Bananas, tangerines, tea, and sugarcane have been successfully introduced into the area. Prospects also look bright for the cultivation of cinchona trees, coffee, pineapples, star anise, lichees, longans, and mangoes. The fertile valleys of the Yarlung Zangbo in Medog County will no doubt soon take their place beside the major zones in China that yield high-value tropical plants.

It seems incredible that this area on the southern slope of Mount Namjagbarwa, which lies on latitude 29° north, well beyond the Tropic of Cancer, should contain all the chief vegetation forms of the humid zones in the northern hemisphere, including even the northernmost tropical rain forest. The reasons for this are manifold.

The actual surface area from the towering peak of Mount Namjagbarwa to the deep valleys of the Yarlung Zangbo is quite extensive. It therefore affords a wide range of climatic conditions and soils suitable for the growth of its diverse flora.

1. A rattan bridge over the lower Yarlung Zangbo in the vicinity of Mount Namjagbarwa. The rattan palm grows profusely in the tropical evergreen rain forest of the southeastern part of the Qinghai-Tibet Plateau. This kind of netted rattan bridge is used to span many of the tributaries and even the mainstream of the Yarlung on the southeastern Plateau.

2. The broadleaf forests of Mount Namjagbarwa are enveloped in mists throughout the year. Their dense canopies prevent light from reaching the ground, which is covered with moss. Climbers and shrubs also grow in profusion, forming thickets that are difficult to penetrate.

The Plateau and serried mountain ranges prevent cold currents from the north from entering this region, so that temperatures do not drop too low. Moreover, the intense solar radiation which exists on the entire Plateau and the warm and humid air masses that blow directly across from the Bay of Bengal raise the temperature of this region considerably.

Mount Namjagbarwa draws many scientists to its slopes on long-term research projects to explore the diverse facets of this lush and attractive part of the Plateau.

4

5

6

3. Mount Namjagbarwa—which towers 7,756 meters above sea level.

4. The *Cirsium heterocephalum*, a species of thistle, grows on humid grassland.

5. Rhododendron bushes at an elevation of 4,200 meters on the south face of Mount Namjagbarwa. Areas from 4,000 meters above sea level upward are classified under the zone of alpine shrubby meadows. Here a great variety of plants thrive.

6. Here Sikkim primroses always flourish by the streams.

7

8

7. Hemlocks festooned with *Usnea*, a type of lichen. Between 1,200 and 2,300 meters of elevation is the home of the evergreen broadleaf forest, where trees of the cupule, magnolia, and camphor families predominate.

8. Fir cones.

9

10

9. A broadleaf forest lying about 2,300 meters above sea level.

10. Because of the heavy precipitation and humidity of the area, every rock here is overgrown with mosses and lichens.

184

11

12

13

14

15

11. Epiphytic orchids in an evergreen broad-leaf forest. An epiphyte is a plant that grows on another plant or object, but is not parasitic.

12. *Dendrobium chrysanthum*, a climber. The foothill tropical evergreen rain forest is found in regions of less than 1,200 meters above sea level. The forest is characterized by a vast variety of tree species and by an abundance of climbers, whose fruit support the rich and varied fauna of the tropics.

13. *Ficus semicordata*, a species of fig. The red fruit in the picture are its hypanthia. They are edible when ripe.

14. *Hedychium parvibracteatum*, a ground flora of the evergreen rain forest.

15. The tiger flower, an undergrowth of the tropical evergreen rain forest. Its wiry calyxes look like the whiskers of a tiger and its white epicalyxes resemble the ears; hence its name.

16

17

16. *Lagerstroemia minuticarpa*, a form of crape myrtle. Its smooth grayish bark predominates in the evergreen rain forest in Medog County in the Yarlung Zangbo valley, about 900 meters above sea level.

17. The *Indofevillea khasiana*, a liana of enormous size found exclusively in this area, grows on slopes 900 meters above sea level in evergreen rain forests.

19

20

21

 18. The *Cyathea*, a genus of tree fern, is a typical plant of the mountain's warmer reaches.

19. With its seed kernel containing 37 percent oil, *Gynocardia odorata*, of the chaulmoogra family, is an excellent oil-bearing woody plant.

20. *Rhaphidophora,* an epiphyte of the tropical evergreen rain forest.

21. A tropical-almond *Terminalia*, a major tree species in the evergreen rain forest.

22

23

22. Plantains. In Medog County grow many kinds of fruit of the tropical and semitropical zones, such as plantains, bananas, oranges, and tangerines, some of them still in a wild state. With proper cultivation, many tropical and semitropical plants of commercial value could thrive here.

23. Wild tangerines.

24

26

25

24. A butterfly poised on a blossom with its wings outspread.

25. The butterfly, leaf-like, is well camouflaged in the foliage.

26. A tree frog of the tropics. It can climb a tree; hence its name.

12 HOME OF WILDLIFE

The vast North Tibet plateau, with its rough, elevated terrain, its rarefied air, and its dry, cold climate, presents too rugged an environment for most of the birds and beasts commonly seen in more hospitable regions of the world. Far from being a place of awesome stillness with hardly any living creatures, however, it abounds in rare species of wildlife.

The largest of the wild animals native to the North Tibet plateau, and the most remarkable, is also the one most commonly associated with Tibet: the yak. The yak has a massive body that may measure as much as three meters long from muzzle to hindquarters, and it may be two meters tall at the shoulders. The highest-dwelling mammal in the world, it is marvelously well adapted to its harsh environment. Its big, heavy head and its body are covered with dark brown hair so long that the thick layers of wool hanging from its flanks flap like aprons as it moves about. Furthermore, it has underdeveloped sweat glands that minimize the loss of body heat. Thus protected from the bitter cold and piercing wind of their natural habitat, yaks can survive on ice or frozen snow, and they may be seen grazing on the North Tibet plateau even in temperatures as low as $-30°$ C.

Although the grasses on which the yak grazes are usually short and sparse, the animal's long teeth and thin lips help it to obtain enough food. The yak's strong legs and solid hooves, soft and elastic on the underside, enable it to travel long distances over rocky, hilly terrain. Its unusual lung capacity enables it to obtain sufficient oxygen from the rarefied air: while the lungs of an Inner Mongolian ox, for example, represent 0.47 percent of its total weight, those of a Tibetan yak account for 1.4 percent of its weight. Although its vision is poor and its view obscured by its shaggy hair, the yak possesses a keen sense of smell which warns it of approaching danger.

Once, as our truck was speeding across the plateau, we somehow inadvertently offended a solitary yak. The beast turned and rushed at us in a fury, smashing our tailgate and propelling the truck violently forward for several meters. Though it will unhesitatingly charge when attacked, the wild yak is not provocative. In moments of danger, the adults protect the young by rounding them up and standing guard beside them, their heads lowered and their huge curved horns pointing in the direction of the enemy. The bull yak is especially bellicose during the mating period, and an unusually strong male may claim as many as ten female partners. This breeding by natural selection tends to ensure the sturdy physique of the next generation and the survival of the species.

During the early Quaternary period, when the climate on earth was much colder than at present and there were repeated major glaciations, the wild yak roamed over large parts of northern Asia and Europe. In more recent geologic periods, however, as the glaciers retreated and the climate grew warmer, the habitat of the wild yak became increasingly restricted. Today it is a rare animal, found only on the Qinghai-Tibet Plateau and in the neighboring regions of Kashmir and Pamir. In China, it has been designated as a protected animal.

Another hoofed herbivore native to the North Tibet plateau is the wild ass, which the Tibetans call "wild horse." It is really neither horse nor ass, though it resembles the one by its speed and the other by its long ears and noisy braying. There are two species of wild asses in the world: the African, which has almost disappeared as a species, and the Asiatic, the latter inhabiting the deserts and grasslands of China and Central Asia. Because the environment differs greatly from one part of this vast area to another, the Asiatic wild ass has developed into three subspecies distinguished by differences in size. The Iranian wild ass is the smallest and the Mongolian subspecies somewhat larger. The Tibetan wild ass is the largest of the three and much taller than the ordinary domestic ass. The dark brown of its upper body contrasts sharply with the grayish-white of the lower half and the inner side of its legs. It has also been designated as a protected animal by the Chinese.

The speed of the Tibetan wild ass enables it to escape its enemies and to seek grazing grounds at great distances from its watering places, which are scarce on the arid North Tibet plateau. Our research team often saw groups of dozens and even hundreds of wild asses running at speeds of up to 60 kilometers an hour. Once, as we were driving through a belt-shaped basin in North Tibet, we encountered a herd of wild asses that darted fearlessly in front of the truck, raced ahead, and then paused nonchalantly until we had nearly caught up with them. The animals repeated this maneuver again and again. Finally they galloped off, apparently satisfied that they had demonstrated their superiority.

How is it possible for the Tibetan wild ass to run so fast at an altitude where the air is so deficient in oxygen? The animal's amazing stamina is probably related to its strong limbs and large lungs, and especially to its well-developed heart. Though a wild ass weighs considerably less than an ox, it has a much bigger heart, the result of evolutionary adaptation to the rarefied air of its environment.

Even swifter than the wild ass is the Tibetan antelope. It weighs only 50 kilograms on the average, but it has a heart as big as that of an ox, and a well-developed nose with extended nostrils. These animals move about in groups of from three to a dozen or more. The males have a pair of black, noded, slightly curved horns, which are about 70 centimeters long and very sharp. We were told of wolves that had had their bellies ripped open by the Tibetan antelope's horns. During the mating period, the male antelope keeps a watchful eye on a strictly guarded group of perhaps a dozen females. Any contender faces a fierce struggle, which more often than not ends in the death of one of the males or the wounding of both.

The horns of the Tibetan antelope, powdered or reduced to an extract, are used as a medicine that Tibetan doctors prescribe for hastening childbirth and for treating goiter, gastritis, and prolonged diarrhea. Like the Tibetan wild yak and the wild ass, this valuable and beautiful animal, which is peculiar to the Qinghai-Tibet Plateau, is listed among China's specially protected wildlife species.

The Tibetan gazelle is seen almost everywhere on the North Tibet plateau. It is much smaller than the Tibetan antelope, weighing only 20 kilograms. The male animal has short horns, while the female has none. When the gazelle runs, the brown hair on its buttocks stands on end, revealing the white underhairs, which look like a disc, clearly discernible from afar.

The blue sheep, found in rocky, cliffy areas, are nimble creatures completely at home on rough terrain. At the approach of an enemy, they make off as fast as they can, with a male in

1. Entellus monkeys live in the subtropical and tropical forests on the south side of the Himalayas, less than 2,500 meters above sea level. They like to move about in groups. The body of an entellus monkey is about 80 centimeters long, and it has a tail about 90 centimeters long, which explains why the Chinese call it "long-tail monkey." Grayish-brown hair grows on its back, on the outer sides of its limbs, and on its tail, while milky-white hair covers its head and breast. The hair on its head is long enough to cover its ears.

the lead of the flock and another bringing up the rear. The argali sheep lives in similar terrain. The male has huge, spiral-shaped horns that coil back toward the ears and then extend to the front.

The North Tibet plateau also has a small number of brown bears, snow leopards, wolves, European lynxes, and other predators. Most of these prey on rodents like mice and hares, but they also attack the smaller hoofed herbivores.

Travelers on the North Tibet plateau often meet with small, chirping birds, such as ground choughs and snow finches, hopping in and out of holes dug by black-nosed mouse hares. This curious phenomenon is explained by the fact that there are few trees or bushes on the plateau to offer shelter from the harsh weather or concealment from the eagles and other predatory birds that often circle overhead. The birds and mouse hares have learned to coexist peaceably in the same home, sharing its protection against their common enemies.

Many kinds of waterfowl inhabit both the freshwater and salt lakes, commonly making their nests on the islands. In July, when we were exploring the western part of the North Tibet plateau, we made an expedition to Bird Isle in the middle of Lake Bangong. We found the island swarming with brown-headed gulls which, frightened by our approach, flew up in such numbers that they darkened the sky. At almost every step we came upon a nest made of waterweeds, usually containing three light-blue eggs with brown spots.

Like the gulls, the bar-headed geese are migratory birds that shuttle between the South Asian subcontinent and Tibet, crossing the Himalayas every spring to make their summer home on the Plateau. The goslings, hatched from eggs three to four times the size of hen's eggs, are raised in the lush grass of lake shores and riverbanks, and by the end of summer are able to follow the adults on their flight south.

In the middle of the Damqog Zangbo, the headwaters of the Yarlung Zangbo, lies a sandbar that is the summer habitat of nearly a thousand bar-headed geese. We found an old Tibetan living nearby who had been assigned by his commune to look after the birds. On condition that the geese were guaranteed normal propagation, he agreed to pick up several

2

4

2. Seen from a distance, the mouse hare looks like a mouse, but it is in fact of the same family as the hare. Unlike a mouse, it has short, round ears and a relatively thick tail.

3. *Phrynocephalus* (toad-headed agamid), a common reptile seen on the Qinghai-Tibet Plateau.

4. The south Asian agama, of the lizard family, abounds in Tibet.

3

thousand goose eggs a year for the commune as a collective earning. The geese had become his good friends, and the cheeping goslings would follow him unafraid as he went about his chores.

The bar-headed geese are prized for their tender, tasty meat, as well as for their down and their eggs. Some families in the western part of the Plateau now raise a few of these birds, or sometimes flocks of them, as domesticated fowl. Certain of the wild mammals can also be bred in captivity for man's purposes. In the vicinity of Lake Bangong, for example, we saw tamed wild asses pulling water carts more effortlessly than horses. And throughout the Qinghai-Tibet Plateau, with the exception of the warmer low-lying areas, domesticated yaks are used for a dozen different purposes, providing meat, milk, hides, and wool, and serving as well for transport and as draft animals.

5

5. The argali sheep are distinguished by their coiling, spiral-shaped horns.

6. A wild yak shot by our scientific research team as a specimen. Its body was found to be 2.2 meters long, its shoulders 1.3 meters high, and its tail 37 centimeters long. Though weighing more than a ton, it was only of medium size among its kind.

7. Wild yaks on the North Tibet plateau. These giant herbivores often roam in herds.

6

7

10

9

11

8. Weighing a red-breasted tragopan. Tragopans live in mixed coniferous and broadleaf forests on the south slope of the Himalayas, less than 3,000 meters above sea level. The male birds, especially, have bright and beautiful feathers. Tragopans are treasured as a rare species: there are only a small number in existence, and these are found in only a few regions of China. Other birds in the picture are: on the bench, two tiny sunbirds (*front*) and a yellow-beaked magpie (*rear*); in the basket on the ground are, among others,

a wheatear, a cuckoo, and a mountain turtledove.

9. These snow finches live together with mouse hares in their holes. The scarcity of trees and bushes suited to nesting creates a housing shortage for the birds, so they are obliged to share the home of another species.

10. Tibetan snowcocks caught by the scientific survey team. Snowcocks are commonly seen in areas under the snow line but

sometimes appear as high as 6,000 meters above sea level, where the ground is covered partly with grass, partly with bare rock. They migrate according to the seasons, but vertically, remaining in the same region.

11. The Tibetan sand grouse lives on the grasslands, meadows, deserts, and semideserts of the Qinghai-Tibet Plateau, at elevations of 4,000 to 5,000 meters. A newly hatched grouse is shown here; an adult bird generally weighs more than 200 grams.

12

13

14

12. The red-faced greenfinches build their nests in bushes.

13. Three newly hatched bar-headed geese, lovable in their downy yellow feathers.

14. As migratory birds, the bar-headed geese come every spring to the Qinghai-Tibet Plateau from south of the Himalayas. The females lay their eggs and hatch the goslings on lake shores. Pictured here are a flock of domesticated bar-headed geese in Ngari Prefecture, northwest Tibet.

15. Brown-headed gulls on Bird Isle in Lake Bangong, Ngari Prefecture. →

16

17

16. The alert Tibetan wild asses are usually seen in the intermontane valleys of the North Tibet plateau.

17. The Tibetan antelope, peculiar to Tibet, is one of the swiftest of the hoofed animals on the Plateau. The male has long, gracefully curved horns that are sharply pointed.

18. A herd of Tibetan wild asses.

18

13
MARVELS OF
HIGH-ALTITUDE
FARMING

In the autumn of 1975, when our research team came to the middle reaches of the Yarlung Zangbo, we smelled everywhere the sweet scent of wheat and rape plant and heard the songs of peasants wafted to us on gentle breezes. We soon learned that an abundant harvest was expected, and the peasants told us with pride of the successes of recent years.

One of the production brigades of the Zaxijicai Commune in Xigaze had reaped 580 kilograms of spring *qingke* barley per *mu* (1 *mu* = 1/15 hectare = 0.1644 acre), setting a national record. The Xigaze Agricultural Research Institute, in its experimental winter-wheat plot, had also set a national record of 836 kilograms per *mu*. Vegetables, recently introduced to the region, had done very well too. There had been good crops of potatoes, the largest specimen weighing a kilo and a half. The heaviest turnip had weighed 15 kilograms, the biggest kohlrabi 20 kilograms, and the sugar content of the sugar-beet crop had exceeded 20 percent.

How could this seeming miracle of farming have occurred in a region as high as the summit of Japan's Mount Fuji, a place where the climate is relatively dry and cold and where even in summer crops may suffer the effects of frost and sudden hailstorms? The answer is that the Yarlung Zangbo valley, like the other agricultural areas on the Qinghai-Tibet Plateau, has two advantages that are of prime importance in farming: long hours of sunshine and a favorable temperature range.

New arrivals in Lhasa are invariably impressed with the azure sky and dazzling sunlight there. Lhasa has an average of 3,022 hours of sunshine per year, whereas Chengdu in Sichuan, for example, at about the same latitude but with a much lower altitude, has only 1,249 hours of sunshine. Like most of the Plateau, the Yarlung Zangbo valley has few cloudy days, even during the rainy season of June, July, and August. In Lhasa, for example, more than 80 percent of the annual precipitation occurs at night. In summer, clouds usually gather in the evening, and rain pours down amid rolls of thunder and flashes of lightning; but at dawn the clouds disperse and the rain stops, heralding another fine, bright day.

This weather pattern means that the crops have sufficient moisture for sturdy growth but also prolonged hours of the

1. These newly transplanted tea bushes are growing apace in a warm and humid river valley of the Hengduan Range governed by the monsoons from the Indian Ocean.

sunshine needed for photosynthesis. Furthermore, the sunshine is intense, because the air is thin and clear on the Plateau, and only a negligible amount of solar radiation is lost in penetrating the atmosphere.

The intense solar radiation causes the temperature on the surface of the plant leaves to be higher than that of the surrounding air, which stimulates photosynthesis. It also warms the soil, especially in summer. This makes it easier for the plants to absorb moisture and nourishment through their roots and particularly favors the growth of tuber and root crops, such as potatoes and turnips.

The strong solar radiation on the Plateau produces an abundance of ultraviolet rays. The ultraviolet rays in sunlight not only help fruits and vegetables to accumulate sugar and synthesize vitamins but also improve their size and color. Small wonder that we found the apples along the middle and lower reaches of the Yarlung Zangbo big, sweet, and tempting. For the same reason, the sugar beets grown on the Plateau contain a higher percentage of sugar than those produced at lower elevations.

Unlike certain other regions on the Qinghai-Tibet Plateau, the Yarlung valley is blessed with a mild climate. The temperature is generally cool, neither extremely cold in winter nor very hot in summer. While certain warmth-loving plants are unsuited to such a climate, others, especially winter wheat, thrive in it.

The relatively low temperature has two beneficial effects for winter wheat. First, it prolongs the growth period, especially during the most important stages of the plant's development: from the appearance of new shoots in the spring to the time of "jointing," and from the formation of heads to the time of ripening. These two stages take a total of thirty to forty days longer on the Plateau than in wheat-producing areas elsewhere in China. This means that the plants have more time for photosynthesis and are therefore able to accumulate more organic matter.

Second, the cool climate protects the plants from the ill effects of excessive heat during the critical final period of

2. A commune member of Deng nationality (*center*) and members of the survey team compare notes on rice transplanting in the subtropical Zayu River valley in the southern section of the Hengduan Mountains.

growth, from the heading stage to maturity. In wheat-producing regions at lower altitude, the high summer temperature at this period reduces the intensity of photosynthesis, while at the same time increasing the plants' respiration activity, so that they consume more of the products of photosynthesis. Heat wilts the leaves and forces the wheat to ripen prematurely. In the agricultural areas on the Plateau, however, even at midday the temperature rarely goes above 20° C, and at night it may drop to 8° C. This range of temperature not only prolongs and intensifies photosynthesis but also reduces the wearing down of its products, thereby promoting the formation of large ears and many, full grains.

The same natural conditions that promote the growth of the crops—strong solar radiation, plentiful ultraviolet rays, and a cool, dry climate—also help to inhibit the appearance and spread of insect pests, thereby contributing to high and stable crop yields.

These favorable climatic conditions are the primary reason for the extraordinary harvests gathered in the middle reaches of the Yarlung Zangbo valley. The ears of winter wheat grown on the Plateau are exceptionally large and full: a single ear may bear forty to fifty grains, while a wheat ear from the North China Plain, for example, bears only twenty-five to thirty grains. Moreover, the individual grains are heavier: one thousand grains from Lhasa or Xigaze weigh 40 to 51 grams, while the same number of grains from Beijing, at the northwestern tip of the North China Plain, weigh only 35 to 40 grams. Consequently, the total yield for each plant is higher: in Tibet's agricultural areas, ten thousand ears of wheat yield approximately 15 to 20 kilograms, as opposed to a yield of 7 to 10 kilograms in the farming districts on the North China Plain. The figures for barley are similar.

Not content with these achievements, the peasants and agro-technicians of different minority nationalities on the Qinghai-Tibet Plateau have experimented with growing various crops at increasingly higher elevations. When a stable yield is obtained for nine out of ten years at a given elevation, they consider that the experiment has been successful. In this way

3. Examining a new variety of *qingke*. Roasted *qingke* flour, called *zanba*, is a staple food of the Tibetans, who mix it with butter or with cow's or yak's milk.

4

they have shown, for example, that corn can be grown at an altitude of 3,200 meters above sea level, winter wheat at 4,100 meters, and spring barley even at 4,400 meters, an elevation close to that of Mount Whitney (4,418 meters), the highest peak in the United States outside Alaska. These figures, among others, represent world records for high-altitude farming.

4. A *qingke* barley field in Ngari Prefecture on the North Tibet plateau. *Qingke* barley was developed from one of the wild varieties. It ripens early, and its relatively short growing time, hardiness, and high adaptability make it grow well at an altitude of 2,500 to 4,000 meters. This field lies at a higher elevation— 4,470 meters—but in a small, sheltered valley where a lake tempers the climate.

5

5. As a native home of barley, Tibet has many kinds of fairly primitive wild barley. This is a new variety found by the research team.

6

6. Giant cabbages grown in the vicinity of Xigaze, 3,800 meters above sea level.

7. In the last twenty years apple trees have been introduced into southern Tibet. Suitable temperature and rainfall, together with plentiful sunlight and ultraviolet rays, make the fruit especially big, colorful, and sweet.

7

218

8. A rich harvest of winter wheat on the Pengbo Farm north of Lhasa, 3,800 meters above sea level.

220

9. Rape plant growing in the Gyirong River valley on the south face of the Himalayas, near the Nepal border. The golden flowers are an irresistible attraction to the research team's photographers.

PINYIN PRONUNCIATION GUIDE

In this book Chinese and Tibetan words are rendered in *pinyin* transcription. In the following pronunciation guide the italicized letter or letters in the "English equivalent" column approximate the sound of the letter or letters in the "*pinyin*" column.

PINYIN	ENGLISH EQUIVALENT
a	h*a*rd
ai	p*ie*
an	w*an*t, except after "y"
yan	between y*en* and me*an*der
ang	*Ang*st (German)
ao	pr*ou*d
e	between tak*e*n and d*u*n
e	*o*ff, after "h" and "k"
ei	*eigh*t
eng	s*ung*
i	between d*i*n and d*ea*n, except after "s," "sh," "ch," and "zh"
(s)i	hidd*e*n
(sh)i, (ch)i, (zh)i }	b*urr*
ia	*ya*cht
ian	between y*en* and me*an*der
iang	h*e* + *ang* (see above)
iao	*yow*l
ie	*ye*s

PINYIN	ENGLISH EQUIVALENT
in	between d*in* and d*ean*
ing	r*ing*
iong	j*ung* (German)
iu	between *you* and L*eo*
o	*o*ff
ong	j*ung* (German)
ou	bl*ow*
u	t*oo*
u	t*u* (French), after "j," "q," "x," and "y"
ua	w*a*nt
uai	w*i*se
uan	w*an*t
uan	t*u* (French) + me*an*der after "j," "q," "x," and "y"
uang	pronounced *wang*, with "ah" sound for "a"
ue	t*u* (French) + y*et*
ui	w*eigh*
un	between *un*der and Ow*en*
uo	t*ow*ard, or *oo* + *wa*lk

PINYIN	ENGLISH EQUIVALENT
b	*b*ought
c	po*ts*
ch*	*ch*alk
d	*d*oor
f	*f*ind
g	*g*old
h	between *h*ot and I*ch* (German)
j*	*j*olt
k	*k*ick
l	*l*ad
m	*m*ight
n	*n*ot
p	*p*ie
q*	*ch*alk
r	between *r*ust and trea*s*ure
s	*s*eat
sh	*sh*ut
t	*t*ear
w	*w*alk
x	between *s*eat and *sh*eet
y	*y*es
z	pa*ds*
zh*	*j*olt

---

*Pinyin "j" and "zh," as well as "ch" and "q," differ slightly in pronunciation: "j" and "q" are dry sounds, pronounced with tongue flattened against the upper palate; "zh" and "ch" are wet sounds, spoken with the tip of the tongue curled up to touch the upper palate.

PHOTO CREDITS

Grateful acknowledgment is made to the following institutes, organizations, magazines, agencies, and individuals whose photographs are included in this book.

Agricultural Machinery Promotion Station, Xigaze (Tibet): Luo Juchun, 163 (2)

*China Pictorial:** Cheng Heyi, 21 (6), 25 (11, 12), 26 (13), 27 (14, 15), 28 (16), 34 (3, 4), 41 (11), 48 (26), 82–83 (16), 110 (4), 110–11 (5), 114 (8), 118 (14), 128 (2, 3), 131 (9), 132 (10), 141 (10), 142 (12, 13, 14, 15), 143 (21), 144 (24), 155 (5), 168 (9), 170 (12), 197 (2, 3), 198 (5), 199 (6, 7), 201 (10), 202 (13), 204 (16, 17), 220–21 (9); Gu Jin, 19 (4); Jia Yujiang, front cover, 60 (11), 99 (8), 145 (26), 168 (8), 195 (1); Li Changjie, 96 (5), 115 (9), 133 (11); Song Xueguang, 48 (27, 28); Sun Yifu, 16–17 (2), 24–25 (10), 56 (5), 134–35 (12); Sun Zhijiang, 18 (3), 130–31 (7), 140 (4), 145 (25), 197 (4), 202 (12), 205 (18); Zheng Changlu, 20 (5), 29 (17), 119 (15), 135 (13), 141 (9), 181 (4, 5, 6), 182 (7), 183 (9, 10), 184 (11, 12), 186 (18), 187 (19, 21), 188 (22, 23), 189 (24, 25, 26), 209 (1), 213 (3), 215 (5)

China's Sports: Wong Yi, 41 (9, 10)

Commission on Multidisciplinary Exploration of the Natural Resources of China:† Guo Changfu, 67 (18); Huang Wenxiu, 154 (3, 4), 155 (6); Li Mingsen, 55 (4), 58 (8), 214–15 (4); Li Wenhua, 171 (13); Sun Honglie, 130 (8), 144 (22), 145 (29, 30); Zhang Mingtao, 35 (5), 71 (1), 72 (3), 75 (4, 5, 6, 7), 76 (8, 9), 77 (10), 78 (11), 79 (12), 80 (13, 14), 81 (15), 84 (17), 85 (18), 107 (1), 108 (2), 109 (3), 112 (6), 116 (10, 11), 117 (12, 13), 120 (16), 121 (17, 18), 167 (7), 178 (1), 179 (2), 180 (3), 185 (16); Zhang Yiguang, 49 (29)

El Popola Cinio (Esperanto edition of *People's China*):* Li Chungeng, 140 (3, 5), 141 (7), 143 (19), 144 (23), 156 (7), 161 (1), 165 (5), 201 (9)

Foreign Languages Press:* Wang Zhengbao, 10 (1)

Institute of Botany, Beijing:† Bao Xiancheng, 143 (17); Chen Weilie, 72 (2), 152–53 (2); Geng Guocang, 21 (7); Lang Kaiyong, 141 (6), 143 (20), 170 (11); Li Bosheng, 143 (18), 201 (11); Ni Zhicheng, 145 (28, 31), 184 (13, 14), 202 (14); Zhang Xinshi, 23 (9)

Institute of Botany, Kunming (Yunnan):† Wu Sugong, 22 (8), 138 (1), 141 (8), 143 (16), 145 (27), 184 (15), 185 (17), 187 (20)

Institute of Geochemistry, Guiyang (Guizhou): Zhang Yuquan, 36 (6)

Institute of Geography, Beijing: Zhang Rongzu, 54 (3)

Institute of Geological Paleontology, Nanjing:† Mao Jiliang and Song Zhiyao, 43 (12, 13); Zhou Sisan and Liang Xiaoyun, 43 (14)

Institute of Geology, Beijing:† Gui Wenli, 46 (22), 47 (25); Pan Yusheng, 45 (19); Zheng Xilan, 44 (17), 45 (18, 20), 46 (21, 23), 47 (24)

Institute of Vertebrate Paleontology and Paleoanthropology, Beijing: Shen Peilong, 32 (1)

Lanzhou University (Gansu):† Li Jijun, 52 (1), 53 (2), 58 (9), 59 (10), 63 (14), 65 (16), 66 (17)

Mountaineering Teams, Commission on Physical Culture: Zeng Shusheng, title page, 100–101 (11)

Nanjing University:† Wang Fubao, 49 (30), 61 (12), 62 (13), 64 (15)

Nationalities Pictorial: Yang Shiduo, 203 (15); Zhang Hesong, 33 (2), 44 (15, 16), 139 (2), 141 (11), 149 (1), 165 (4), 169 (10), 211 (2)

New Sports Magazine: Chen Leisheng, back cover, 99 (9), 125 (1)

People's China (Japanese edition):* Zhang Jiaqi, 113 (7)

People's Liberation Army Pictorial: Wu Shouzhuang, 218–19 (8)

Popular Science Film Company, Shanghai: Li Wenxiu, 166 (6), 182 (8)

Publicity Department, Chengdu Military Area: Huang Daoming, 157 (8)

Publicity Department, Tibet Military Area: Li Jun, 37 (8)

Qinghai Daily: Hu Luyi, 129 (4, 5, 6)

The Sports Gazette: Zhang Xiaojing, 94 (3), 95 (4)

Xigaze County (Tibet) Agricultural Bureau: Kong Fanzhi, 216 (6)

Xinhua News Agency: Cheng Zhishan, 37 (7), 88 (1), 200 (8); Guan Tianyi, 57 (7), 92 (2), 98 (7), 100 (10), 164 (3); Gu Shoukang, 216–17 (7); Wu Ming, 57 (6), 97 (6)

Xinjiang August First College of Agriculture: Zhang Xinshi, 23 (9)

---

*Of Foreign Languages Publishing and Distributing Bureau.
†For the Multidisciplinary Research Team of the Qinghai-Tibet Plateau, Chinese Academy of Sciences, which team included specialists from several institutions.

INDEX

Italicized page numbers indicate the location of illustrations.